AF517929

## ADVANCE PRAISE FOR THE BOOK

'This book is an extraordinary tour de force on the inspiring life and phenomenal contribution of an outstanding jurist, independent thinker, engaging scholar, transformative institution builder and a truly remarkable leader—Justice Syed Mahmood. Justice Mahmood's journey of engaging with law, justice, institutions and most of all with truth and power made him one of the tallest figures of his time. But what makes him even more special is that he did all of this with honesty, integrity and rectitude, while maintaining humility and grace. The authors, Mohammad Nasir and Samreen Ahmed, should be thanked, appreciated and celebrated for their painstaking research and account of the trials, tribulations and joyous journeys of Justice Mahmood. They have reflected through this compelling work their passionate commitment to the story of Justice Mahmood, while maintaining the intellectual rigour and scholarly adherence to the discovery of facts along with his evidence-based opinions. The book is a fantastic read and the authors have done a yeomen's service to posterity by writing this fascinating book and recording forever the story of an outstanding judge who was ahead of his times. Justice Mahmood's contributions may have been forgotten by history, but we would not have been forgiven, but for this work, which has done justice, albeit delayed, but thankfully, not denied.'

Professor (Dr) C. Raj Kumar, *Founding Vice Chancellor, O.P. Jindal Global University*

'As generations pass, the difficult labours of biographers become even more complex. Mohammad Nasir and Samreen Ahmed have successfully recalled for us the heroic life of Justice Syed Mahmood—the first Muslim and the first North Indian judge to be elevated to the High Court of Allahabad. His greatness was acknowledged by Chief Justice Hidayatullah to be in his "greatness of his pronouncements, the greatness of his intellect, the greatness of his knowledge and the greatness of his mind. He was great in every trait which a judge must possess." Justice Mahmood had only six years on the Bench when he resigned rather than be dependent on the "smiles and the frowns of the British Chief Justice". Chief Justice J.S. Verma hailed him as an activist and incandescent justice recognized as a first activist judge who "treated the law as a living organism"—a "spirit in which judges engage in activism even today". Justice Mahmood left an indelible impression on almost all arenas of judicial interpretation.

'Well-archived in the book is "his role in the colonial transformation of education and its reconciliation with the issue of Muslim identity and its intellectual and cultural heritage as such". However, the authors offer this biography as neither a hagiography nor an apologia. A major achievement of this critical biography is to reanimate "the values of religious tolerance, composite culture, inter-faith understanding and mutual respect" which Justice Mahmood embodied. In these virtues lie the present and the futures of Indian constitutionalism.'

Professor (Dr) Upendra Baxi,
*Emeritus Professor of Law, Universities of Warwick and Delhi*

'An excellent biography of a towering legal luminary of 19th-century India who had the courage and conviction to differ from the powers of the day for the sake of justice. Justice Mahmood's acumen and steadfast quest for justice continues to be an inspiration for the judges of today, enabling them to ward off all attacks against their independence in upholding the values ingrained in our Constitution.'

Justice Badar Durrez Ahmed, *Former Chief Justice, Jammu and Kashmir High Court*

'History is often written from and for the time in which it appears. But it is rare to come across a work whose exposition of a judge's career, lived almost a century ago, is of such immediate relevance. This account of Justice Syed Mahmood's intellectual and moral courage has many lessons for the present. It is a welcome addition to the writings on the Aligarh movement and the Indian judiciary.'

Dr Farhan Nizami, *Director, The Oxford Centre for Islamic Studies, and The Prince of Wales Fellow, Magdalen College, University of Oxford*

'A dissenting judge writes an opinion knowing fully well that his opinion is not going to be the law. But he makes an appeal to the future. Justice Syed Mahmood is widely appreciated for his dissenting opinions which in subsequent years were accepted as correct interpretations of law. This book is a praiseworthy effort to familiarise the legal fraternity about the contribution of this great judge. Incisively written, this book is a must-read for anyone interested in the judicial process and legal history.'

Professor (Dr) Faizan Mustafa, *Vice Chancellor, NALSAR University of Law, and President, Consortium of National Law Universities*

'A seminal figure who transcended great tribulation in unpredictable times has been brought to life by this scholarly book. The book succeeds in restoring in the annals of history the extraordinary life of Syed Mahmood before it fades into the mists of time. The celebration of this forgotten hero is a commendable step towards providing inspiration to the present generation of lawyers and history enthusiasts.'

Sanjiv Saraf, *Founder, Rekhta*

'This brilliant biography of an icon is also a fine depiction of the liberation of the Indian mind from foreign fetters. Justice Mahmood, a quintessential luminary of the early Aligarh vision, nurtured the important concept that judicial independence was a necessary precursor to political freedom. The first Indian judge of the Allahabad High Court became a beacon for judicial activism when he challenged an English Chief Justice who had turned the court into a parade of his "smiles and frowns". This superb work does justice to law by resurrecting Syed Mahmood's receding memory.'

M.J. Akbar, *author and Member of Parliament, Rajya Sabha*

'In the sands of time, on the path of dispensation of justice, we cannot fail to notice the large footprints left by Justice Syed Mahmood. This marvellous book must be read by all the judges and jurists of India to appreciate the courage and hard work required to deliver true justice. In the quest for justice, a judge has to learn to face adversities and many a time swim against the strongest of tides. The dissents of Justice Syed Mahmood against white judges enforcing British justice in India was an act of exemplary courage.

'In the one and a half centuries of the history of the Allahabad High Court, we hardly find any judge of equal brilliance, presiding with extraordinary knowledge and understanding of civil, criminal and personal laws. His clarity of the first principles of law and its application to explain the complex legal issues led to the path-breaking texts of law which treated jurisprudence as science.'

Justice Sunil Ambwani, *Former Chief Justice, Rajasthan High Court*

SYED MAHMOOD

# SYED MAHMOOD

*Colonial India's Dissenting Judge*

Mohammad Nasir
Samreen Ahmed

BLOOMSBURY
NEW DELHI • LONDON • OXFORD • NEW YORK • SYDNEY

BLOOMSBURY INDIA
Bloomsbury Publishing India Pvt. Ltd
Second Floor, LSC Building No. 4, DDA Complex, Pocket C – 6 & 7,
Vasant Kunj, New Delhi 110070

BLOOMSBURY, BLOOMSBURY INDIA and the Diana logo
are trademarks of Bloomsbury Publishing Plc

First published in India 2022
This edition published 2022

Copyright © Mohammad Nasir and Samreen Ahmed, 2022

Mohammad Nasir and Samreen Ahmed have asserted their right under the Indian Copyright Act to be identified as the authors of this work

All rights reserved. No part of this publication may be reproduced or transmitted in any form or by any means, electronic or mechanical, including photocopying, recording or any information storage or retrieval system, without the prior permission in writing from the publishers

This book is solely the responsibility of the authors and the publisher has had no role in the creation of the content and does not have responsibility for anything defamatory or libellous or objectionable

Bloomsbury Publishing Plc does not have any control over, or responsibility for, any third-party websites referred to or in this book. All internet addresses given in this book were correct at the time of going to press. The author and publisher regret any inconvenience caused if addresses have changed or sites have ceased to exist, but can accept no responsibility for any such changes

ISBN: HB: 978-93-54353-08-6; e-ISBN: 978-93-54354-66-3
2 4 6 8 10 9 7 5 3

Typeset in Fournier MT Std by Manipal Technologies Limited
Printed and bound in India by Thomson Press India Ltd.

FSC www.fsc.org MIX Paper from responsible sources FSC® C010615

To find out more about our authors and books, visit www.bloomsbury.com and sign up for our newsletters

## CONTENTS

# FOREWORD

Justice Syed Mahmood was a remarkable man of his time. Like many other educated upper-class Indians of the day, he went to England for his higher studies. He was enrolled in Cambridge, from where he did law. It was expected from the son of Sir Syed Ahmad Khan to be well educated, but Mahmood made his name in history as a judge of the Allahabad High Court, which he was for a short period of six years, between 1887 to 1893. The Law Reports of this period are full of the opinions of Justice Mahmood that were given in a variety of fields of law, such as Hindu Law, Muslim Law, Transfer of Property, Criminal Law, amongst others. Justice Mahmood made his mark as a Judge not just due to his learning or his genius, but because of his sense of equity, justice and fairness, and as an eminent jurist had said, for keeping human being at the centre of his judicial philosophy. In my opinion, Justice Mahmood was great because of his judicial approach, for his distinct ability to come out with a fresh, often bold, perspective on law.

During my initial days of practice at the Allahabad High Court in late 1980s and early 1990, it was often that I heard the name 'Mahmood' from senior advocate Gur Dayal Srivastava. It was he who told me how a judgment authored by young Mahmood as a District & Sessions Judge of Raebareli reached the Privy Council and how the Members of the Judicial Committee of the Privy Council were impressed by the judgment and enquiries began on Mahmood, which ultimately led to his elevation as a Judge of the Allahabad High Court—the first Indian to be elevated as a Judge of the Allahabad High Court. Although he became a permanent Judge in the year 1887, prior to that, from 1882 onwards—when he was barely 32—he thrice officiated as a Judge of the Allahabad High Court.

Though there is no space here to discuss his judgments, yet I may refer to one particular case, just to make my point. This is his dissent in *Queen Empress Vs Phopi* (1891). Under the old Criminal Procedure Code, as it was applicable at that time (i.e. in 1891), the word 'hearing' was to be interpreted as given under Section 423 of the Code. The common practice in the Allahabad High Court at that time was that if a convicted person has appealed to the high court and is not there in person before the court, nor is he represented by a pleader, yet if the Judge of the high court has gone through the records of the case, that would qualify as 'hearing'. This obviously seemed odd to Justice Mahmood, who referred the matter to the Full Court.

The Full Court consisted of four Judges, which included the Chief Justice John Edge and Justice Mahmood. The majority opinion 3:1 upheld the earlier practice. Justice Mahmood dissented and held that there is no 'hearing' unless and until the appellant is either present in person to argue his case, or is being represented by a lawyer. He observed as under:

> I think it necessary for me to say that if it is true that the law of British India makes it possible for me sitting here as a Judge, in the first place, by dint of my writ to order a person to be imprisoned and tied by a chain, then in the next days to require the mockery of giving him notice, the mockery of asking him to attend, when I, by dint of the exercise of my own power had made it impossible for him to attend, and then have the solemn mockery of having his name called out. If this is the law of British India, I hope the sooner it is abrogated the better.

Justice Mahmood said this in 1891 when there was nothing like Section 303 or Section 304 of the present Criminal Procedure Code, which makes it a right of a defendant to be represented by a lawyer and a duty of the court to provide legal assistance to the one who is not represented by a lawyer. Nor was there anything like the State Legal Services Authority.

Justice Mahmood never lost sight of the practical difficulties the litigants faced, and even 140 years back in time, he was thinking about a fair access to justice. It is relevant here to record the point which Justice Mahmood made in those early days, and this is not contained in any of his opinions but is a part of the minutes of Justice Mahmood, which he drafted to be introduced before the Parliament for giving more power and jurisdiction to the high courts. Justice Mahmood emphasised the question of language and the fact that many Indians were not confident in either speaking the English language or getting a translated copy of the record available in the court. In those days, it was common practice for an appeal to be dismissed without hearing on the sole ground that the appellant had failed to translate the record of the case into English. Justice Mahmood's recommendation was as follows:

> I think in view of the vast population which will be affected by the rules or practice as to enforcing translations, the matter is sufficiently significant to be taken in hand by the government which is responsible for the peace and administration of the country, rather than be left to considerations relating to the convenience of the judges. The truth is that the rules as to translations into English involve so considerable an expense on the part of litigants that they practically amount to imposing a tax upon the litigant population and I am afraid in some cases amount to a denial of Justice. I say this with due respect for the opposite opinion. The costs of these translations become costs in the cause, so that a rich litigant is practically free to swell the costs of litigation against a poor man by getting the record translated even in petty cases.

There are competent judges and good judges, even eminent judges, but there are very few who are judged by posterity as 'great Judges'. Justice Mahmood was a great judge, and to see the reasons as to why he was a great judge, we only have to refer to what Justice M. Hidayatullah, former chief justice of India, said of Justice Mahmood:

> His greatness lay in the greatness of his pronouncements, the greatness of his intellect, the greatness of his knowledge and the greatness of his mind. He was great in every trait which a judge must possess. 'To be perfectly just', says Addison, 'is an attribute of the divine nature; to be so to the utmost of our abilities is the glory of man'. Syed Mahmood was great in the sense of a judge's oath to decide cases to the best of his ability, knowledge and judgment.

Distinguished lawyer and former Advocate General of Uttar Pradesh, Dr. K. L. Misra, at the unveiling of the portrait of Justice Mahmood at the Allahabad High Court on 27 November 1966, said:

> My Lord, the greatness of this court, the glories of this court are, in a large measure, due to Mahmood. If I were to make a selection today, if there was any kind of comparison of the judiciary of this high court, the judges of this court with the judges of the other great courts in the world, and if I had to select a delegate who would represent this high court, nay the courts of our country in an international assemblage of judges, past and present, I would unhesitatingly choose Mahmood.

This book is an effort to define the legacy of Mahmood and it provides an engaging perspective on why Mahmood deserves a fuller examination. It would be a surprise to many that so far there was no biography on Justice Mahmood. Drawing upon archival as well as secondary sources, the book presents a nuanced narrative of a great Indian Judge. The book will be a thoughtful companion for anyone interested in reading about Mahmood's intriguing personality and his contributions to law, education, literature and interfaith understanding.

I congratulate Mohammad Nasir and Samreen Ahmed for remembering Justice Mahmood the way he should be remembered. Through a book.

Sudhanshu Dhulia
*Chief Justice, Gauhati High Court*

## ACKNOWLEDGEMENTS

Coming in the midst of a pandemic, this book has had an exceptionally tortured gestation. Amongst the known, the recalled and the missed, the list of those to whom it owes debt is much longer than the few names that will appear. This compels us to chart an escape, fastened to an apology—sorry, if we have missed out on thanking you individually.

As the manuscript wandered towards the status of a book, many distinguished friends, teachers and colleagues were generous to a fault in helping cajole thought into a sustainable viewpoint: Naved Masood, former secretary to the Government of India and a veteran *Alig*, shared detailed insights on the first draft of the manuscript, which helped polish the chapters, and remained a pillar of support till its completion; Atul K. Thakur, literary consultant and columnist, lent constructive suggestions to make this book engaging for a wider spectrum of readers besides supporting its publication; Rasheed Kidwai, visiting fellow at the Observer Research Foundation, guided us on the nuances of publishing; Prashant Jha at the *Hindustan Times* enthusiastically gave space for an opinion piece on Syed Mahmood's birth anniversary on 24 May 2021, which serves as a summary of the book; Shafey Kidwai, noted scholar of the Aligarh Movement, critically examined the chapter on AMU; and M.J. Akbar, author and parliamentarian, gave a near-final draft of the manuscript a once-over and pointed out errors.

The book benefitted from the occasional help and feedback of many: the one and only Professor Upendra Baxi, senior lawyer Parag P. Tripathi, Justice Sunil Ambwani, Justice Badar Durrez Ahmed and the teachers in the faculty of law, AMU. We remain obliged to the Public Relations Office, AMU and Rahat Abrar for giving us copies of pictures in their possession.

The book required an enormous amount of research of archival material related to colonial law and history. In this endeavour Syed Hussain Haider, archivist at the Sir Syed Academy, and support staff at the archives section of the Maulana Azad Library were invaluable in helping with digging up digitized documents related to the subjects of enquiry. Thanks are also due to the university librarian, the library staff at the faculty of law, AMU and India International Centre for their unstinted cooperation with locating research material.

Which finally brings us to express gratitude to Bloomsbury for its trust, the editorial team under the able guidance of Praveen Tiwari and Nitin Valecha for nurturing the book with vigour and commitment through the publishing process, Shreya Chakraborti and Rashi Gupta for doing so much to complete the editing and background work, Syed Dilshad Ali for designing a marvellous cover and Nilanjana Dey for taking care of the niggles in the proofs.

Right now we cannot think of any way to repay the debt of those named and, no less important, the unnamed. But eventually we might have to. So the relief is only temporary!

# Introduction

The impetus for this book came during the centenary celebrations of the Aligarh Muslim University (AMU) in 2020. Speaking at the programme of the centenary celebration of AMU—one of the oldest and largest educational institutions in India—Prime Minister Narendra Modi called on the AMU community to undertake research on lesser-known national heroes of India as we approach 75 years of Independence. The year 2021–2022 represents a significant moment on the cusp of history of both India and AMU as we have AMU at 100 coinciding with India at 75. Subsequently, the Sir Syed Academy, AMU urged me to author a biography of Justice Syed Mahmood.

As is said, a book one writes gestates for years in the mind, and indeed on bookshelves, with the embryo forming and reforming, sometimes still, sometimes alive, sometimes kicking. In this sense, the story of this book is a culmination of a long journey that began much before the first word was written, and it takes me back to my rookie days in law school. Interestingly, my introduction to Syed Mahmood is owed to Justice Sudhanshu Dhulia Sahib, who in 2009 was a puisne judge of the high court of Uttarakhand. He requested me to arrange for him the literature related to Justice Syed Mahmood at AMU, for not only did he deeply admire his legal and judicial scholarship but he was also intrigued by his personal life story. I enthusiastically collected a large amount of literature from different libraries and individuals in Aligarh and handed it over to Dhulia Sahib over the years. On a lighter note, I confess to withholding a part of my collection every time I visited him in Nainital, so that I could get a further opportunity of an audience with him, with 'additional literature on Mahmood' being the ruse! It is befitting that Dhulia Sahib has now written the foreword for this book.

This exercise gave me an opportunity to read more deeply about Justice Mahmood. Prior to that, I had a smattering of knowledge about him as a student who read the textbook briefs of his judgments on Muslim law.

A useful tip I learnt from this—almost no information is ever useless. Back then, I stored it away in a corner of my mind, with an insurance of a notebook, or as we know these days, a computer cloud! Never did I know it might be of such relevance.

So what is the vantage point for reading Justice Mahmood in India's legal history? The role of law in advancing justice, as understood in colonial India, was different from what we understand today under a democratic constitution. The link between the two is to be found in the integrity of fearless Indian judges during the colonial era who provided us with a framework of an independent judiciary. However, like the majority of things, the most remarkable form of change goes unnoticed when its embers are first lit. Back in the 19th century, Mahmood became perhaps the first judge to resist colonial power by espousing the cause of judicial independence. It was a change colonial India needed then—a drastic change of mindset. And it was a change whose enduring value may not have been felt then, but surely needs to be remembered now.

Mahmood left his mark in legal history through the eventful years when he was a judge of the Allahabad High Court. At the time, it was the highest position a native could hold in the British Government of India. He was the first Indian Muslim and first north Indian to be appointed to any high court in India, apart from being the first non-European member of the Allahabad Bar. At the age of 32, from 1882 onwards, he officiated as a temporary judge of the Allahabad High Court on four different occasions, before eventually becoming permanent in 1887. He served till 1893 when he resigned under dramatic yet acrimonious circumstances as a response to his differences with Sir John Edge, the then chief justice of the Allahabad High Court, who was intolerant of Mahmood's independent views. As a truly independent judge, Mahmood could not accept judgeship being dependent on the 'frowns and smiles' of a British chief justice. Sir Syed, his father, saw his resignation as an act of 'Englishmen robbing Indian civil servants of their self-respect', but was proud that his son had mustered the courage to stand up to the British.

The judiciary in the colonial regime was considered the weakest branch of the state as it possessed neither the power of the purse nor the power of the sword. In spite of this constraint, the role of the judiciary has in no way been inferior to the role of the executive and legislative branches in the evolution of India's legal system. In fact, owing to India's common law credentials, the judiciary has been more influential than other branches of the state in the development of certain areas of our legal system. In this role, too, Justice Mahmood established himself as a son of India whose nonpareil judicial endowments were a source of inspiration to the entire Indian legal fraternity. A study in his legal scholarship is a study in the wealth of the nation. While he is most reputed for his metier in Muslim law,* his judicial scholarship sparkled in other areas of law as well. His pronouncements on Hindu law not only widened the grounds for Hindu widows for claiming maintenance but were also useful in drawing the legislative framework of the Hindu Marriage Act, 1955—the modern codified Hindu law governing marriage and divorce. He was at his

* The term 'Muslim law' is erroneously used interchangeably with 'Islamic law' or 'Muhammadan law'.

To a great extent, there is an overlap, and to some extent, difference between Islamic law and Muslim law. Islamic law means the entire body of law in its pure form, called *shariat*, derived from sources such as the Koran, the teachings of the Prophet, the opinion of jurists, etc. Muslim law refers to that part of Islamic law that is applied as a personal law to Muslims in India. The law as applied to Muslims in India is at variance with Islamic law as it has been modified by the law of the land, customs and usages.

Muhammadan law is the same as Muslim law; rather it is a misnomer, which has been used popularly. The book has used the term Muslim law instead of Muhammadan law, except where reproducing quotes from the text of another author, such as by Justice Mahmood in his writings. The book is conscious of the nature of the phrase to be used, keeping in mind the above nuances.

original best in interpreting provisions of the Indian Evidence Act, 1872 in all branches of law—even more so in Criminal law. His innovative approach is all the more remarkable as the 1872 legislation essentially incorporated the common law, and was thus a distilled outcome of centuries of rulings of the English courts.

Justice Mahmood's contribution to the development of law in colonial India through his activism is echoed far and wide. Justice Michael Kirby, former judge at the high court of Australia from 1996 to 2009 and a great dissenter himself who also served as the president of the International Commission of Jurists, in his lecture on 'Judicial Activism', has quoted Justice Jagdish Sharan Verma, former chief justice of India. Crediting Justice Mahmood for sowing the seeds of judicial activism in India, Justice Verma had said:

> The judiciary will continue to respond to the changing needs of the times. That is how activism has evolved. Let me dispel the popular impression that judicial activity began less than two decades ago. The truth is, way back in the 19th century, Justice Mahmood of the Allahabad High Court delivered a dissenting judgment which sowed the seed of activism in India. It was a case of an undertrial who could not afford to engage a lawyer. So the question was whether the court could decide his case by merely looking at his papers. Mahmood held that the pre-condition of the case being 'heard' (as opposed to merely being read) would be fulfilled only when somebody speaks. Just look at how that man treated the law as a living

organism. That is the spirit in which judges engage in activism even today.[1]

Imagine those days of the last quarter of the 19th century where judicial subservience to the political regime—more significantly, that of a native puisne judge to an Anglo-Saxon Chief Justice—was considered a natural order of things under the imperial government. Justice Mahmood was the only Indian among the British judges in the high court. Even while he was only a temporary judge of the high court, he wrote dissenting judgments with vigour and fearlessness, as someone far more knowledgeable than his British counterparts. As an Indian judge of standing in colonial India, it sometimes exemplified his burden of double consciousness—having to think as an Indian judge in British India—and one almost senses the strain of overthinking.

The adulation for Justice Mahmood's dissents has never been stained, or strained, by doubt. Speaking at the sesquicentennial celebrations of the Allahabad High Court on 13 March 2016, Justice Dhananjaya Yeshwant Chandrachud, judge of the Supreme Court of India at present, remarked on Mahmood's dissents, 'Justice Syed Mahmood's judgments in dissents show a strength of character and values.'[2]

Justice Rohinton Fali Nariman, judge of the Supreme Court of India who retired in August 2021, has done a thorough study of all the dissenting judgments[3] of the Supreme Court of India in his two-volume *Discordant Notes: The Voice of Dissent in the Court of Last Resort* (2021). Notwithstanding that the book focuses on the dissenting judgments of the Supreme Court of India and some of its judges who have gone down as *Great Dissenters*,[4] Justice Nariman, before dealing with the dissents of the *Great Dissenters*, first pays tribute to Justice Mahmood. He writes:

> Before dealing with the dissents of these (great dissenters of the Supreme Court), it is important, at this juncture, to pay a tribute to a fearless Indian judge—Justice Syed Mahmood—who had to pay the price for his dissenting judgments in the colonial climate of the Victorian era, in that he was forced to resign as a high court judge because of the ego of his English chief justice, who refused to tolerate any disagreement with his views by the only 'native' on the bench.[5]

Justice Nariman, in his book's introductory chapter, 'The Need for Dissent', makes a scholarly analysis of dissenting judgments from a philosophical point of view and embarks upon a general discussion on the pros and cons of dissenting judgments. He concludes by observing that the pros of dissenting judgments far outweigh the cons.[6] Justice Mahmood's select dissenting opinions, examined in Chapter 4 of this book, flesh out the intrinsic value of dissenting judgments in a legal system, and hence pulsate with the arguments advanced by Justice Nariman in favour of dissenting judgments. They also reveal the various ways in which he dissented. At times, his dissents were absolute—disagreeing with the reasoning as well as the decision of the majority, and sometimes only limited—concurring with the decision but not the reasoning.

To begin with, Mahmood demonstrated 'judicial integrity' through dissent and represents one of the earliest examples of this. On how dissent manifests in judicial integrity, Justice William Douglas, a former US Supreme Court judge known for his dissents, put it thus, 'It is the right of dissent, not the right or duty to conform, which gives dignity, worth, and individuality to man.'[7]

Mahmood's dissents are rooted in the conviction that dissenting opinions are important tools in the development of law in a way that leaves room for further developments. By pointing out flaws in the majority judgment, a dissenting opinion proposes remedial that may be applied in the times to come. That Mahmood was endowed with a judicial acuity far ahead of his times is evinced by the fact that a number of his dissents were later accepted by the courts, and continue to be the law of the land. Towards this, his dissents, which later became the basis for overruling the majority judgment, served as a kind of safety valve for the courts to internalise error prevention. In this sense, he represented what former Chief Justice Charles Evans Hughes of the US Supreme Court referred to dissent—as 'an appeal to the brooding spirit of the law, to the intelligence of a future day, when a later decision may possibly correct the error into which the dissenting judge believes the court to have been betrayed'[8] or what another fine US Supreme Court judge, Justice Benjamin Cardozo, remarked as 'the voice of the majority may be that of force triumphant, content with the plaudits of the hour and recking little of the morrow. The dissenter speaks of the future, and his voice is pitched to a key that will carry through the years.'[9] William Douglas put it rather succinctly, 'Dissents or concurring opinions may salvage for tomorrow the principle that was sacrificed or forgotten today.'[10]

As recently as in 2020, a three-judge bench of the Hon'ble Supreme Court of India comprising Justice Sanjay Kishan Kaul, Justice Aniruddha Bose and Justice Krishna Murari in its judgment in the case of *Raghunath (D) v. Radha Mohan (D) and Others*[11] quoted with approval the judgment of Justice Mahmood in *Gobind Dayal v. Inayatullah*.[12] Not long before that, in the Supreme Court's landmark judgment in *Shayara Bano v. Union of India*,[13] wherein the practice of triple-talaq was declared unconstitutional, Justice Rohinton Nariman quoted the following extract from Justice Syed Mahmood's judgment in Gobind Dayal's case, 'It is to be remembered that Hindu and Muhammadan laws are so intimately connected with religion that they cannot readily be dissevered from each other.'[14]

However, the subsequent approval of a number of his dissents is not to suggest that his dissenting opinions were always correct. Many of them were not approved later, just as they were not approved then.

Mahmood's most famous dissents are the ones for upholding human rights in the Victorian era—such as on the 'concept of fair trial' in *Queen Empress v. Pohpi*[15] and against the 'torture of prisoners for extracting confessions' in *Queen Empress v. Babulal*.[16] Through them, he called attention to the grim impact which the majority judgment can have on individual liberty and on society generally. His dissenting opinions on these issues made out a case for engendering principles of justice in the interpretation of law, even if there is an absence of a precedent or practice in favour of the same.

His dissents also kindled debate on the finer points of law which, in some cases, improved the majority opinion, especially in cases of Muslim law. Although Mahmood's style of writing did suffer from prolixity to a certain extent, his dissents were characterised by clarity of thought and coherence, unlike some majority opinions, which were broadly worded, being a product of compromise and accommodation of the views of colleagues.

Moreover, as some of his dissenting opinions were relied upon by courts in foreign jurisdictions, such as in Pakistan, Malaysia, Bangladesh among others, it also brings to the fore the value of dissents to legal developments in foreign jurisdictions.

As an intellectual giant in his own right, Mahmood was endowed with the ability to raise questions and define, represent and articulate new thoughts and perspectives. His judgments laid the path for a renewed sense of scholarship in his times, for erudition always floated in the air, leavened by his vintage quest for a reason to confront orthodoxy and dogma.

Edward Said's comments in 1993 on who an intellectual is describe Mahmood aptly:

> There is a trend that the figure or image of the intellectual might disappear in a mass of details, and that the intellectual might become only

> another professional or a figure in a social trend. What I shall be arguing in these lectures takes for granted these late-nineteenth century realities originally suggested by Gramsci, but I also want to insist that the intellectual is an individual with a specific public role in society that cannot be reduced simply to being a faceless professional, a competent member of a class just going about his/her business. The central fact for me, I think, that the intellectual is an individual endowed with a faculty for representing, embodying, articulating a message, a view, an attitude, philosophy or opinion to, as well as for, a public. And this role has an edge to it, and cannot be played without a sense of being someone whose place it is publicly to raise embarrassing questions, to confront orthodoxy and dogma (rather than to produce them) . . . and whose raison d'etre is to represent all those people and issues that are routinely forgotten or swept under the rug.

One can certainly argue with conviction that Syed Mahmood was among the leading intellectuals of his times, with dissent as the raison d'etre of an intellectual. Furthermore, if the intellectual's task is to represent those people and issues that are routinely swept under the carpet, then Mahmood performed this task admirably through his scholarship, which placed humanity at the centre of his legal universe.

One need not go beyond the words of the great former Chief Justice M. Hidayatullah, who encapsulated Syed Mahmood's standing as a judge in the following words,

'Anyone who wishes to name six greatest Indian Judges of all times, must find it difficult to omit the name of Syed Mahmood from his list. It is indeed a moot question how far he will go in his list before he must name him . . .'[17]

In a similar vein, a noted book on Indian judges titled *Indian Judges: Biographical and Critical Sketches* published by Natesan and Company, Madras mentions, 'Syed Mahmood was perhaps one of the greatest judges who ever presided over a Chartered High Court in India.'[18]

Nevertheless, the enthusiastic adoration of Mahmood as a 'man of law' makes his engagements with other domains of knowledge less known to the readers. Outside of law, this book seeks to document his role in the colonial transformation of education and its reconciliation with the issue of Muslim identity and its intellectual and cultural heritage as such. Over the years, as I peeped through the window of history of the making of AMU, I realised that Mahmood's role is not as widely read and written about as it perhaps deserves to be, mainly because it has been overshadowed by and hyphenated with that of his father, Sir Syed Ahmad Khan—the founder of AMU and a great social reformer of 19th-century India. As a result of a lukewarm dissemination of his contribution to the making of AMU, it appealed to me to somewhat fill this space. I have attempted to de-hyphenate his role from that of his father while insisting that his father's accomplishments would not have seen fruition in the first place without his assistance.

By analysing the lesser-known works, deliberations and interventions of Mahmood in setting up the Muhammadan Anglo-Oriental (MAO) College, the forerunner of AMU, Chapter 2 of this book interrogates the role of Mahmood in spelling out what constitutes a university. His emphasis on the intellectual enlightenment of students, with higher education as a pivot that grooms generations of youth of the country to contribute to the intellectual advancement of civilisation, resonates with India's much acclaimed National Education Policy of 2020. Mahmood's intellectual engagement with education continued with greater vigour after his resignation as a judge and led him to write his magnum opus, *A History of English Education in India*—a work that is still widely regarded as one of the most objective, insightful and in-depth analyses of the education system followed by the British in colonial India.

Beyond law and education, Mahmood also ponders on the values of religious tolerance, composite culture, inter-faith understanding and mutual respect. The last chapter of this book makes an appraisal of this. Whereas lesser men found conflict in the rich diversity of life, Mahmood was big enough to see the essential unity behind all diversity. He was critical of Aurangzeb's wanton disregard for pluralism, and preferred the enlightened ideas of Dara Shikoh, the eldest Mughal prince and a victim of Aurangzeb's conspiracy, that mosques as well as temples mediate a single candle's light. He envisaged Hindu–Muslim relations based on confident partnership in a cultural and spiritual diversity where divisiveness would be its betrayal. While nobody can deny that he was tethered to the cause of 'Muslim education', it was not a divergence from the broader mission of instilling scientific temper and rationality through modern education among all Indians. The impetus on Muslim education stemmed from the fact that Hindus had embarked on modern education and reforms much before Muslims.

Nevertheless, a biography is no hagiography and certainly no apologia. It would be misleading to frame our views on Mahmood's personality or his relationship with the Raj only through the prism of his judicial valour, which no doubt was commendable and came at a great personal and professional cost to him. There were instances, particularly during the early part of his career, where he pledged allegiance to and expressed solidarity with the Raj, sometimes bordering on servility. But it was seemingly more driven by personal considerations—to garner political patronage of the government for the education institution he helped his father establish, and for his own advancement in the civil service and judiciary—rather than by conviction. Such instances, in what appear to be inconsistent and contradictory with his judicial behaviour, are discussed in Chapter 2, on his contributions in education, and Chapter 3, charting his professional career in law.

Chapter 3 also discusses in length the infamous tussle of Justice Mahmood with Chief Justice Sir John Edge—an episode that has prodded commentators to elevate him to the status of a legend in the annals of Indian legal history. The book relies upon archival letters to scrutinise threadbare the remonstrance and counter-remonstrance between Mahmood and the Chief Justice. In contrary positions based on right and righteousness, it is easy to take sides—and taking sides with the protagonist of the book is quite tempting. An unsentimental appraisal of the controversy with full facts is therefore imperative.

The Chief Justice's intolerance of contrary views by a 'native' puisne judge was the root cause of the tension. However, some of Mahmood's errant personality traits, such as impetuous behaviour, resulted in his disappointment turning into outrage, which brought in an element of vehemence in his response. The angry retorts would have obviously tilted the scales in a fight between the Anglo-Saxon and the native when the missives would have been perused by other Anglo-Saxons outside the judicial realm. It is good to remember that curtailment and understatement of emotions were the hallmarks of the Victorian era English prose to which celebrated English littérateurs of the time—like Lytton Strachey, founder of the Bloomsbury group[19]—drew attention almost contemporaneously.

The fight between a 'British Chief Justice' and a 'native puisne judge' of the high court was something that would be looked askance at by the decision-makers in the highly hierarchical, possibly even stratified, institutional frameworks of the time. When the puisne judge was a native, the tendency to err on the side of the higher British authority was almost instinctive. The protagonist was adjudged at fault by the temper of the Raj in the twilight decade of the 19th century.

In the course of history, the shelf life of some luminaries was short. Many wobbled on the slippery perch of alcoholism. After his resignation from judgeship, Mahmood's excessive indulgence in alcohol—to an extent that it became a disease—incapacitated him from work and estranged him from family and friends. Given his accomplishments and meteoric rise, the final part of his life, captured in Chapter 5, reads a dispiriting tale. He died at the age of 53. Writing about him in 1973, his great-granddaughter Scheherazade Tilat Alim fittingly summed up his life: 'Anguish and disappointment are no strangers to an artist, and Syed Mahmood was no exception. His life was a strange blend of triumphs and tragedy, the triumphs are as dazzling as the tragedy is dark.'[20]

The book presents a narrative of Syed Mahmood's life and his contribution to the consciousness of post-1857 India. In seeking to provide a holistic window on his life and works, the book has benefitted from the major attempts made in this direction earlier.

In 1973, the Faculty of Law, AMU dedicated a special volume of the *Aligarh Law Journal* to a study of Justice Syed Mahmood. Aptly titled *Mahmood Number*, it commemorated the contribution of a scholar–judge who was a prime mover of legal education at MAO College. The dedication conveys this as much:

In loving memory of
late Mr Justice Syed Mahmood
'Master of Law and Master of Language'
to whose deep interest in legal studies
the Faculty of Law
Aligarh Muslim University
owes its genesis and nurturing
is dedicated
this Fifth Volume of the Aligarh Law Journal
in
humble gratitude

The editor's note said:

> The Faculty is fully conscious of the fact that one volume of its annual publication is no adequate repayment of its debt to him [Syed Mahmood]. However, it takes great pleasure in dedicating Seventy Years and Six Months after his sad demise on 8 May 1903, this special number of the Aligarh Law Journal to his revered memory in the hope that by focusing the attention of scholars on him as an ardent reformer, a brilliant educationist, an accomplished writer, an erudite lawyer and a great judge, it may stimulate further research in, and writing about, his rich contribution to the areas of law, education and study of languages in India.

Contributors to the journal include some of the most eminent personalities in law drawn from the bar, bench, academia and civil servants. Notable are pieces by Hon'ble Chief Justice M. Hidayatullah (former chief justice, Supreme Court of India), 'Justice Syed Mahmood'; Hon'ble Justice S.N. Dwivedi (former judge, Supreme Court of India), 'Mahmood's Contribution to Humanitarianism in Law'; Hon'ble Justice V.R. Krishna Iyer (former judge, Supreme Court of India), 'Mahmood's Relevance and Greatness Illustrated with Reference to a Muslim Matrimonial Law Case of *Abdul Kadir v. Salima*', Professor V.S. Rekhi (former dean, Faculty of Law, AMU), 'Mahmood's Opinion in Janki Case: A Study in Activism'; and Prof. S. Misbahul Hasan (former dean, Faculty of Law, AMU), 'Mahmood and the Muslim Law of Legitimacy'.

The pre-eminence accorded to the *Aligarh Law Journal* in the pantheon of legal periodicals in those days was succinctly described by the All India Reporter, which reviewed its maiden issue: 'If the example of the Law Faculty of the Aligarh University is emulated by the law faculties of other universities, we are sure, a day will not be far off, when we will have our Storys, Salmonds, Pollocks and Diceys.'

The authors also reviewed a booklet running into 56 pages carrying sparse details of Mahmood's life titled *Tazkira-e-Syed Mahmood* (Narrative of Syed Mahmood) by Mohammad Ameen Zuberi. Written in Urdu with a sprinkling of Persian lexicon, the publication is a thumbnail profile of Mahmood spread across eight essays of six to seven pages each, most likely meant for school curriculum. The booklet does not carry the year of publication, but according to some historians of the Aligarh Movement, it was published prior to Independence.

In 2005, the Sir Syed Academy, AMU came out with a compilation of Syed Mahmood's papers in a book titled *Justice Syed Mahmood's Papers* edited by Iqbal Hussain, professor of history at AMU. The papers are crucial for understanding Syed Mahmood and some phases of the Aligarh Movement beginning from 1893. The book's strenuous efforts to reproduce papers as they existed in the original despite many of them being brittle, torn and difficult to read are laudable.

The most important and exhaustive work was done by Alan M. Guenther in his PhD thesis titled 'Syed Mahmood and the Transformation of Muslim Law in British India'. It was submitted in 2004 to the Institute of Islamic Studies of McGill University in Canada. This is a valuable work that has examined the role of Indian Muslims in the transformation of Muslim law under British rule through the lens of Mahmood's contribution in this field.

This book partly takes inspiration from the seeds sowed by these and other writings on Mahmood by expanding on the thread laid down by them. It also makes an effort to fill the gaps that were left by the earlier works. To give one such instance, in the *Aligarh Law Journal Special Volume*, one will not find any commentary of Mahmood's ruling in *Amir Muhammad Khan v. Jafri Begam*[21] that heralded an important judicial reform on Muslim law relating to the administration of estates. This is covered here in the chapter on his judgments. But given Mahmood's wide range of intellectual corpus, this book naturally rules out the narration of 'Syed Mahmood's life and works beyond the barest skeleton'. Instead, the book has tried to synthesise various accounts on him and add another layer to the framework for looking at the major strands of his personality, judgments and life episodes, which may whet the appetite for further research.

A glance at the table of contents shows the simple route map of the book—the story of Syed Mahmood through his life years and his contributions permeating through it. As such, and in view of the foregoing discussion, I do not feel the need to present a separate precis of each chapter as in a formal introduction. Mahmood's engagement in education preceded his career in law, and therefore, has been taken up first. The only aberration to this vertical arrangement of chapters is the final one.

Whilst the theatre of discussion is the socio-political context of 19th-century India, wherever possible, the book spotlights the contemporary relevance of his judgments and works of historical importance. To cater to a wider group of audience, the chapter on Mahmood's landmark judgments has attempted to present his scholarly yet very dense and lengthy judgments in lucid style. This turned out to be the most challenging task.

The book is intended for general readership, besides students and scholars of law, modern India, education, colonial India, interfaith and religious studies, literature, biography and South Asian studies.

MOHAMMAD NASIR

1

# The Journey Begins: Childhood, Education and Family

## Early Life and Education

The date 24 May 1850 marks the birth of an extraordinary individual—judge, intellectual, poet, legislator, philanthropist and academician—Syed Mahmood.

The sociocultural life at home often plays a major role in shaping our cognition, where everyday musings leave a lasting impact on formative brains and contribute towards building the thought process. The same is true of Mahmood. A true embodiment of his name, Mahmood,[1] an Arabic word meaning 'praiseworthy' or 'laudable', he demonstrated diligence and perseverance punctuated by an inquisitive mind in his early training. Born in Delhi as the second child to Sir Syed Ahmad Khan and Parsa Begum, alias Mubarak Begum, he was a charismatic and well-bred child. His parents imbibed in him the values of careful utterance, humility in language, reverence for elders and indebtedness to teachers.

*Syed Mahmood in his teens*

While much is known about Mahmood's father, Sir Syed Ahmad Khan, the information on Mahmood's mother and the marital life of his parents is scanty. Neither Mahmood nor Sir Syed have made notable allusions to Parsa Begum in their writings, and Sir Syed's early biographers, George Farquhar Irving Graham and Khwaja Altaf Husain Hali, make only nominal reference to her. From whatever minimal information is available, she is known to have been a benevolent woman. After the First War of Independence in 1857, the north-western provinces[2] faced an acute drought. Sir Syed, a judicial officer posted in Moradabad then, was entrusted by the government with the task of overseeing the relief services. While Sir Syed's role was indeed appreciated, it came across as rather surprising when Hali, in his biography of Sir Syed, *Hayat-i-Jawed*, admired the role of Parsa Begum as 'more benevolent, than him'. He writes:

> Besides this relief centre, Sir Syed himself and his wife, who was more benevolent than him looked after the poor and destitute. At his house, bread and curry were distributed among the destitute daily . . . Sir Syed had also accommodated 4-5 such boys and girls in his house who were being looked after very kindly by Sir Syed's wife.[3]

Syed Mahmood had his bismillah ceremony[4] at the age of four years, four months and four days with a reading lesson of the Arabic alphabet of the Holy Koran. He undertook lessons in Koran at a *maktab*[5] run by his maternal aunt in Delhi. Hafiz Abdul Rahim, a well-known poet and author, was employed as his private tutor to school him in Persian and Arabic while he was in Delhi.

The Revolt of 1857 hugely impacted the life of Indian Muslims, and Syed Mahmood was no exception. He says that Indians witnessed the worst phase from 10 May 1857 till September, and it was only in 1858 that things began to move towards normalcy, including his education. Describing the turbulence in his life caused by the Revolt of 1857, he wrote:

> I had not nearly finished the Koran and had begun to learn Persian when the disastrous events of the great Mutiny occurred on the 10th of May 1857 at Meerut, and the Sepoy Mutineers took possession of Delhi the next day perpetrating the horrible atrocities of a general massacre of Europeans including women and children described at pages 567 and 571 of Vol. III of Beveridge's *History of India*.

> I well remember the horror and consternation and terror which seized the whole fortified city of Delhi . . . whole of that period and for months afterwards all my studies were stopped, Delhi having been taken by storm on the 14th September 1857 and the whole city captured by the 20th September 1857. It was indeed not till 1858 when my father had been appointed Principal Saddar Amin [sic] of Moradabad the highest judicial office then open to my countrymen that I resumed any studies of the Koran and Persian language.[6]

Mahmood resumed studies in 1858 after a gap of almost a year when he, along with Sir Syed, moved to Moradabad where the latter was appointed as the *sadr-amin* or the chief commissioner. On reaching Moradabad and finding a lack of proper schools there, Sir Syed formed a committee to manage a small Persian language school and enrolled Mahmood there. There, he continued taking lessons in the Koran and Persian and Arabic languages.

In 1860, realising the grave consequences of the mutiny, especially for Indian Muslims, and understanding the importance of the English language in post-mutiny India, Sir Syed planned to send Mahmood for higher education to England. Mahmood was influenced by his father's counsel, which was layered in the exigencies of time, about the importance of adding the study of English language to his study of the Koran, Persian and elementary arithmetic.[7]

In fact, Sir Syed's first tryst with English education was the education of his own sons. His elder son, Syed Hamid, was born in 1849, a year before Mahmood. To orient them to the educational pattern of the West, he hired a tutor at the salary of ₹100 per month to teach his sons Hamid and Mahmood for three and two hours, respectively. Hamid had lesser disposition towards education than what his father had desired. Sir Syed often expressed his consternation on Hamid's lackadaisical attitude towards studies, saying, 'Hamid hardly devotes himself to studies.' There is no record available of Hamid's formal educational qualifications. Despite this, he supposedly did enough to make the grade as sub-registrar in Banaras and deputy superintendent of police during the later part of his career. Like his father, Hamid was also known for his caring nature, but alcohol addiction and consequent divestment from his father's affection are believed to have sown the seeds of an inferiority complex in him, making him bitter in dealings. Hamid left the ephemeral world on 30 January 1894 at the age of 45.

Sir Syed's third and youngest child was a daughter named Amina. While the family's outlook towards women's education was certainly ahead of its times, it was seemingly not enough for English education. Whatever may have been the case, unfortunately, she died young in 1870 at the age of nine. During the time of her death, Mahmood, along with his father and brother, had already begun his voyage to England.

Under the circumstances, Syed Mahmood was the first in the family to have been schooled in the English language and colonial curriculum. During his mid-teens, he had become proficient enough to present the English versions of his father's lectures to the Scientific Society of Aligarh.[8]

In 1862, at the age of 12, Syed Mahmood was bereaved by the death of his mother. The event is understood to have brought an upheaval in his life. After this, Syed Ahmad migrated to Ghazipur (now in eastern Uttar Pradesh) and appointed a Bengali tutor, also known as *bangali babu*, who taught English to Mahmood. Another man, who was assigned the task of translating *Tabeen-ul-Kalam*[9] into English, was engaged for honing Mahmood's English vocabulary. The influence of private English tutors was apparent in young Mahmood's early choice of readings—Lord Tennyson, Carlyle and Charles Dickens. As a child prodigy, he mastered arithmetic and advanced literature together.

In 1864, Syed Ahmad was transferred to Aligarh. Here, Mahmood was enrolled at the Government Anglo-Vernacular School, now known as Naurangi Lal Government Inter College. Four years later, in 1868, Mahmood moved to Banaras, where he was admitted to Queens' College, which was widely reputed at the time as a seminary of English language and literature. There, Mahmood had the benefit of the tutelage of the distinguished Anglo-Sanskrit scholar and poet Ralph T. Griffith, the famous translator of the Ramayana in English and author of the collection of poems collection in *Idylls from the Sanskrit*. Queens' College was envisioned as an alchemy of the Banaras Sanskrit College and the English Seminary. It adhered to a unique integrated pattern of education, conscientiously assimilating the knowledge of the East and the West.[10] Coincidentally, its educational philosophy and ideals mirrored those of Sir Syed Ahmad Khan and are believed to have largely shaped Mahmood's views on education. Meanwhile, alongside his studies in college, his relationship with oriental learning continued at home under the supervision of a learned private tutor of Arabic.[11]

*The Government Anglo-Vernacular School, Aligarh, where Syed Mahmood enrolled at the age of 10 (it has since been renamed Naurangi Lal Government Inter College)*

Sir Syed's emphasis on inculcating a scientific temperament amongst the students at MAO College applied to his son too. The speech delivered by the

14-year-old Syed Mahmood at the Scientific Society[12] on 16 August 1864 bears testimony to this. Etched in prolific authorship and oratory, the speech came to be widely acclaimed in later years. Walking his talk on the need for education, Mahmood demonstrated his commitment by contributing ₹5 and ₹10 to the Scientific Society library and building fund, respectively. He made another speech at the Scientific Society Institute on 14 February 1866, which was reported in the inaugural issue of the *Aligarh Institute Gazette* of March 1866.[13]

During a mushaira (poetic symposium) in Delhi, 15-year-old Mahmood read out a ghazal (short poem consisting of rhyming couplets) in Persian with precision—an extraordinary feat for a young boy of his age. It amazed the audience, which included the famous poet Mirza Ghalib, who is reported to have risen from his seat and kissed Mahmood's forehead in appreciation.

*Kante bichana na rah mein aaiye hasrat-e-visal*
*Nazuk hain rah ravani ghareeb alvaton ke panon*
—Syed Mahmood's ghazal in Persian[14]
Do not lay thorns on the path, O' wistful yearning
(for the beloved)
Delicate are the feet of those who travel in exile
(Translated by Azarmi Dukht Safavi)[15]

*Mahmood with family and friends of his father, Sir Syed Ahmad Khan (Standing left to right): Syed Hamid (elder brother), Mulazim Chajju (attendant), Syed Mahmood, Syed Zainul Abdein (judicial officer, Ghazipur), Mirza Bundo (attendant) (Sitting left to right): Maulvi Imdad Ali (deputy collector, Cawanpore), Raja Jai Kishan Das (deputy collector, Hathras), Sir Syed Ahmad Khan (father), Rahmat Khan (deputy collector, Bijnore), Rai Baldev Baksh (deputy collector, Moradabad)*

## Higher Education

By 1868, Mahmood had passed the matriculation examination of the Calcutta University from Queens' College. His academic excellence shone through as he stood first in the order of merit and scored high in English and Arabic—almost equalling the maximum marks allotted. Subsequently, he got selected as one of the nine students from all over India to be conferred with a government scholarship for the sons of native gentlemen of rank and position to study in England to prepare for the Indian Civil Service examinations or the professions. His performance merited him with a double scholarship at Cambridge, England. The scholarship grant included the amount of ₹6,000 for tuition fee and residence, and ₹3,000 for the two-way journey. After this, Mahmood's ship sailed to England.

Whilst Syed Mahmood was studying Latin and other subjects required for his admission to Cambridge, he was also proactively helping his father in his research and writing. Although there were other people involved in assisting him, his son was markedly his most prominent aid. Mahmood had the opportunity of visiting the libraries of the India Office and the British Museum while assisting his father in the collection of materials for Sir Syed's book titled *Life of Mohammed and Subjects Subsidiary Thereto*, popularly known as *Essays on the Life of Muhammad*. The title of the book in Urdu is *Khutbat-e-Ahmadiya*.

The noted American scholar David Lelyveld affirms this while referring to Sir Syed's work *Essays on the Life of Muhammad*. He writes:

> *Essays on the Life of Muhammad* was something more than a translation of Khutbat-i-Ahmadiyya, the Urdu 'original' that was published many years later. The traces of Syed Mahmood's studies and lengthy quotations in Latin from Horace, and in English, from Pope, the references to a wide variety of European texts, were none of them accessible to Syed Ahmad Khan. The title page states, 'The original English text of these essays has been revised

and corrected by a friend,' an odd, if attractive, thing to call one's own son.[16]

In 1870, Mahmood joined the Christ's College of Cambridge University in the Michaelmas term.[17] He was joined there by Anand Mohan Bose,[18] who, despite being barely two months senior in enrolment to Mahmood, endearingly referred to him as 'my tutor in undergraduate'. Mahmood's stay at the university in England was marked by a robust engagement in the rich cultural and literary life of the university, which he held close like a treasure for the rest of his life. He participated in a number of literary gatherings where he often met Tennyson and Carlyle and attended the story-reading sessions of Charles Dickens. Mahmood was present at the last story-reading session of Charles Dickens, shortly after which Dickens fell ill and died in June 1870.

He also participated in the Cambridge Union debates. On one occasion, he moved the motion, 'in the opinion of this House, England has failed in her duties to India.' A.M. Bose is said to have supported this motion with a rousing speech that carried the day with a vote of 74 to 26.[19]

Mahmood prepared for the Bar alongside his studies at the Christ's College. He was called to the Lincoln's Inn and got himself attached to a practising barrister named John Pearson, who was later appointed the Queen's Counsel.

For a year, he also took instructions in Greek and Latin. Later in his life, when he became a judge, he invoked these in his judgments, which stood out for their in-depth comparative analysis of legal systems.

He performed admirably in his annual exams in 1871 at Cambridge, securing 10th position, and was tied for the first place in the English language paper. He contributed two articles to the Cambridge College magazine *Fleur-de-Lys* and also penned a prize-winning essay. In one of his pieces, 'A Brief Sketch of the Rise and Progress of Islam', he presented a sketch of pre-Islamic Arabia and the life of Prophet Muhammad (P.B.U.H.) till *hijrah* (migration) to Medina, and cited his father's *Essays on the Life of Muhammad* while mentioning that its copies were available in the libraries of the Union Society and Christ's College. While still a student at the Christ's College, he also delivered a lecture at the Royal Asiatic Society of London[20].

This was the grandeur of the so-called non-English-speaking debater. He successfully laid to rest the erroneous notions of capability about the Indians travelling to England. Resonating this, a professor of Christ's College acknowledged the potential of Mahmood while remarking that he shall 'Blaze as a bright star in the firmament of law.'[21] Later in his career as a judge, Mahmood wrote in a letter dated 8 September 1893, addressed to the Hon'ble J.D. La Touche, chief secretary to the government of the North-Western Provinces (NWP) and Oudh, 'I have spent years of labour with any advantage to acquire the English tongue in which I [sic] won the English Prize at Christ's College, Cambridge, as long as 1871.'[22]

In fact, the issue of representation of Indians in the imagination of the English as found in the books then piqued Syed Mahmood; particularly the depiction of manners and customs of Indian races highlighting their purported ferity. As per an account of Sir Syed,[23] when a young Englishman approached Mahmood and asked him whether he was a Hindustani, he was embarrassed to identify himself as such and had quickly added that his ancestors had formerly been of another country.

This incident ignited the fire in young Mahmood to change the perception about Indians. In a speech at the public dinner during the foundation-laying ceremony of MAO College in January 1877, he is reported to have said that both Englishmen and Indians stood on the same pedestal as subjects of the Queen of England and submission to Her Majesty made them equal in status.[24]

In an article Mahmood wrote for the *Calcutta Law Review* in 1879, he remonstrated the use of the expression 'our Indian subjects' employed by common Englishmen exclusively for the people of a colony of the British Crown—India. The differential treatment meted out to Indians—in contrast to the people of Canada and Australia, also a part of the British empire and for whom no such expression was used—was found to be discriminatory, derogatory and violative of the exclusive privileges of the crown. Mahmood wrote:

> Our 'Indian subjects' is an expression which, in a speech from the throne, or in a royal proclamation, would not be out of place; but in the mouth of Englishmen who, like ourselves, do not breathe the

> atmosphere of sovereignty, the expression sounds as an attack upon 'the divine rights of kings', and a violation of the exclusive privileges of royalty. That the expression is commonly used cannot be denied, that it is never intended to have the sense in which we have interpreted it, gives it a significance greater than the importance of a mere verbal discussion. India is not the only dependency of the British crown; Canada and Australia are as much portions of the British empire as any part of India. But we do not remember even hearing Englishmen employ the expression 'our subjects' towards the people of Canada or Australia.[25] . . .
>
> It hardly lies in the mouth of Englishmen to use contemptuous language towards us, because we helped them to build the empire over which they hold sway; it is hardly befitting to give us the invidious name of their 'subjects' because we helped to bring about the supremacy of which they have become the owners.[26]

Underlining the importance of semantics as vehicles of thought and not mere rules of grammar, he postulated that the difference of language, though apparently merely a verbal one, is in reality of greater consequence than a simple rule of grammar or use of idiom. As language is considered to be the vehicle of thought, and thought as the basis of human action, then expressions in ordinary use indicate not only the feelings of Britishers who use them, but also their behaviour towards Indians. 'The behaviour of Englishmen towards the people of this country is a circumstance of which the eloquent patriot of the day often complains, which English philanthropy of the nineteenth century often denounces,'[27] he wrote.

Lamenting that the consequences of the fallacy of the expression 'Indian subjects' culminated in the relations of Englishmen with Indians becoming a matter of national antagonism or of personal insult and provocation that result in unbounded injury to public feeling, he made an impassioned case to the Raj for respecting the sentiments of national morality by recognising Indians as 'fellow-men'. He appealed:

> The legislature is abused; complaints are sent up to Parliament; Parliament only lends an indifferent ear to Indian questions, and vociferous clamour, thus defeated, finds shelter in the guise of whispered grumbling. If it is an infallible law of nature that there is no effect without a cause, that every cause is in its turn itself an effect of some other cause, the present state of feeling between the ruling race and the ruled must have adequate causes, causes which cannot be said to be conducive to the welfare of the British rule or the prosperity of India.[25]
>
> Let Englishmen, instead of assuming the vainglorious name of 'conquerors', do justice to historical truth and national morality, to humanity and civilization, by recognizing, not only in words but in deeds, the millions who inhabit the vast continent of India, as their fellow-men, fellow-workers, and fellow-subjects.[27]

While it remains a bit of a mystery as to why Mahmood did not fully complete his Cambridge degree,[28] he successfully qualified as a barrister[29] when he returned to India on 26 November 1872. At that time, his father Sir Syed was posted as the judge of the small causes court in Banaras. The city of Banaras, along with his family and friends, gathered to celebrate the occasion, and to honour the first Muslim barrister of India. Mahmood lived with his father in Banaras before moving to Allahabad to begin his professional legal career. He frequently visited Banaras until Sir Syed retired and permanently settled in Aligarh in 1876.

According to Lieutenant Colonel Graham, the event is a landmark in the history of NWP (British India). He writes, 'When Syed Mahmood returned from Cambridge and Lincoln's Inn as a barrister at law, his father gave a dinner to celebrate the occasion. It was remarkable as being the first dinner in these provinces at which Mohammedan and English gentlemen sat down together.'[30]

The dinner was presided over by Alexander Shakespeare (then commissioner of Banaras) and toasts were raised in his honour. Barrister Mahmood candidly spoke of his wish:

> To unite England and India socially even more than politically. The English rule in India, in order to be good, must promise to be eternal; and it can never do so until the English people are known to us as friends and fellow subjects, than as rulers and conquerors.[31]

Mahmood had profound love for his alma mater and left an Eastern mark on the Western world by instituting two prizes of £200 at Christ's College, one each for Arabic and Persian. His love for oriental languages grew stronger. He also wrote two essays in Urdu for *Tahzib ul-Akhlaq* (the Muhammedan Social Reformer); one on *dosti or* 'friendship'[32] and the other on *shiddat-i-itqa* or 'severity of piety,'[33] after his return from England.

## Unravelling Mahmood's Intellect and Persona

As we narrate in the later part of the book on Mahmood's genius in law, one should know that it was not his only forte. Outside the court of law too, his was a very much sought-after company. His intellectual craft and wit sparkled in informal environments. Blessed with a memory and diction par excellence, he once left his contemporary Sir Tej Bahadur[34] awestruck by reciting 30 stanzas of Tennyson's *In Memorium A.H.H.* by rote, the book that was in Tej's hand. On another occasion, he recited a number of verses from Firdausi's *Shahnama* and displayed an extraordinary knowledge of pandits[35] in his recitation of the Ramayana. In many of his lectures and public events, he was popular for using figures, lines and symbols for denoting notions and pleasantly surprising his audience. Once, to illustrate the rise and fall of English education amongst the Indian Muslims, huge diagrams, alarmingly painted in red and green, were prepared on the working principle of mercury in a thermometer.[36]

Mahmood believed in the young, particularly in young students, to an extent that would have been remarkable in any age. The *Aligarh Institute Gazette* carried the recollection of a young mind who had the benefit of Mahmood's nurture.

> . . . His interest in the 'younger generation' was great, but it was of a peculiar nature. I am speaking of a time when he resided in Aligarh and was in the best state of his health. Supposing you were a young mind who had a liking, say, for mathematics. On a morning you make up your mind to see Mr. Mahmood. You enter his study—a spacious hall, whose roof looked as if it was supported, at least on two of its sides, not upon walls but upon book-shelves only. You are asked to take your seat, and after a few polite enquiries, if you are not actually preamble, enacted and codified, you at least find and are made to learn a definition of yourself according to the nature of studies you were pursuing.[37]

After noting that in the present instance, the young man in question was a student of mathematics, the recollection continued:

> . . . Now after a short silence followed by a smile, is opened a series of easy questions to which you readily answer and feel yourself very scientific.
>
> Question: Tell me, my friend, the result when you divide a number or anything denoting a number by itself?
>
> Answer: One.
>
> Question: What is X divided by X?
>
> Answer: One.
>
> Question: But supposing the value of X is zero, then you will say that zero divided by zero is also one?
>
> Answer: Y. . . Ye. . . Yes.
>
> Question: Now tell me what is 50 divided by 50?

> Answer: One.
>
> Question: Quite right; but I suppose you remember the axiom—things equal to the same thing are equal to one another.
>
> Answer: Certainly, Sir.
>
> Question: Therefore, according to your own answers, 50 is equal to zero, which is impossible, hence, it is shown that things equal to the same thing are not necessarily equal to one another. What do you say to that?
>
> Answer: No reply.[38]

The young man concluded his quagmire in the following words, with a sense of what was to expect in the next one:

> Any attempt on your part to gainsay what you have already said is of no avail—the laws of deposition being stern. Similarly, in your next visit, in spite of your being very careful this time, you confess that part is greater than the whole, and so on to the great amusement of your cross-questioner (Mahmood) [sic].[39]

Understandably, Mahmood's bemused audience often remarked that hearing him on any topic was a recipe for greatest possible mental strain. For an absent-minded person before him, he did not seem to care much. But even the most intelligent people were reduced to absent-mindedness in no time! Resistance against his attractive genius could not be envisaged. The *Gazette* further commented:

> Just think for a moment of a high grade brain-power, say a hundred horse power strong working full steam upon the feather intellect of an average man—a dead dry leaf of ignorance in a storm of learning and erudition. And so we were and he—a peaceful lion who loved to play with mice. But peaceful only when he was playing.[40]

Mahmood's fondness for multilingual literature and poetry, especially Persian and Urdu, remained integral to his literary repertoire. Not only did his recitation of choicest couplets enthral informal gatherings but he also used it to good effect to unwind himself in solitude. The sittings for sweet conversation *sukhana-i-shireen* were long—longer for the subject—even longer than the poets' night of sorrow—'sans wine, sans song, sans singer, and sans end'. In the course of satiating his audience, he also revelled in tutoring them on the fundamentals of poetry. When speaking how a line in poetry was divided into feet, he cautioned '. . . but gentlemen, you should never attempt to convert these feet into yards or poles'. In another instance, while explaining the rudiments of English prosody, he said, '. . . in reading aloud let your consonants be pronounced as audibly and clearly as in writing it is required of you to draw definitely and faithfully the outlines of each letter in a word.'[41]

One finds allusions to Sufi-influenced Persian couplets in some of his writings and speeches. During his tenure of judgeship, he frequently visited famous Persian poet, Mirza Sanjar Tehrani, and spent hours in his company reciting poetry. His proficiency in Urdu was manifested in his ability to simplify even the most convoluted Urdu write-ups.[42]

The *Aligarh Institute Gazette* captured Mahmood's erudition, as described in the words of a person who immensely benefitted in Mahmood's company:

> Perfect humour, keenest wit, producing most pleasant surprises, deepest learning with immense powers of comprehension and analysis—of crushing and grinding down the hardest matter into its last atom of atoms—these were some of the characteristics of a giant mind and a mighty intellect. Call me imaginative if you like. But do not facts put an end to imagination? If so, then let me say that the greatest living fact ever experienced by me in my student life which called forth greatest awe and highest respect was the late Mr. Syed Mahmood.[37]

Mahmood had a resplendent personality, and in spite of handling the jigsaw puzzle of professional responsibilities at various points in his career, he was able to balance the 'professional' and 'personal' with care. Mahmood's heart was benevolent as much as his brain was bright and his mind was sharp. Satish Chandra Banerji, a noted lawyer, politician and public intellectual of pre-Independence India, who worked with Mahmood as a junior lawyer, recollects how his senior, Justice Mahmood, attended to him when he was down with fever in September 1896. Writing in the *Hindustan Review*, later reproduced in the *Aligarh Institute Gazette*, he wrote: I was down then with an attack of high fever, but I still remember with loving gratitude how Mr Mahmood who had his bed in another room would come five or six times in the night to feel my pulse and stroke my forehead.[43]

Hali mentions that Mahmood acquired the quality of munificence from his mother, and practised it till his last breath. This is endorsed by Mohammad Ameen Zuberi, who sketched Mahmood's life in his short booklet *Tazkira-e-Syed Mahmood*. As per his account, Mahmood was committed to the values of philanthropy and made generous donations to those in need, much more than expected.[44] In fact, later in his life, Mahmood was known to always keep a chequebook in hand for rescuing those in need. Satish Chandra Banerji also bears witness to this quality of Mahmood. Commenting that Mahmood embodied the spirit of *what you spend on a friend and comrade is gained*, he wrote:

> One word I must say here about Syed Mahmood's liberality and his generosity of heart. Nobody, I believe, ever approached him with a petition who did not get more than he wanted. Mr Mahmood seems to have acted upon the theory that money was earned only with the object of being given away and his cheque book was always at almost everybody's service. Another thing very characteristic about him was his hearty laughter. He was a very jovial man, whose heart was quite as large and as tender as his intellect was acute and bright. You could not have a better and kinder friend.[43]

Banerji also wrote that the first thing that struck him about Mahmood was his culture—not only did he come across as a well-read and well-informed man but also as a thoroughly cultured gentleman. Ameen Zuberi writes that Mahmood's popularity in social circles stretched far and wide, and that a notable visiting Aligarh would invariably call on him.[45]

Percy Wallace, a British professor who taught English literature at MAO College, spoke of Mahmood's geniality after meeting him.

> He is one of the finest men I ever met, both inside and out . . . He is . . . a fine broad shouldered man with a genial manner and a big way about him altogether . . . He speaks English with almost incredible precision of idiom and I certainly never listened to a more interesting talker. He smokes cigarettes incessantly.[46]

## Marriage and Family

Syed Mahmood's wedding was solemnised on 28 February 1888 at Aligarh with Musharraf Jahan Begum—also known as Mahmoodi Begum—daughter of Khwaja Ashraf Uddin Ahmad Khan and grand-daughter of Sir Syed's uncle Nawab Khwaja Zainul Abidin Khan. The ceremony was graced by the family and close friends. Mahmood, serving as Allahabad High Court judge then, did not hold his *walima* (feast), and the estimated amount of ₹ 500 was donated to MAO College.[47]

Syed Mahmood lovingly addressed her as 'Jan-e-man Musharraf', and gifted her a palatial house, presently known as Sir Syed House,[48] AMU, in dower. A portion of the Sir Syed House premises, which was the private dwelling of Musharraf Jahan Begum, was called Pili Kothi. She was known to be skilled in the acquisition and disposal of immovable property as well as shares. The property presently houses the Centre for Continuing and Adult Education, AMU.

Mahmood's wife was a formidable figure, and her aura is portrayed by Masood Mukhtar in his work *Harf-e-Shauq* when he visited her residence:

> I saw Mahmood Begum once in my childhood. I went to Pili Kothi with my mother. As we entered through the door, we were greeted by a distinguished *Mughalani* [feminine of attendant] and a few trees laden with *Harsinghar* [coral jasmine] flowers. *Gautakia* [cushions] were laid on the *takht* [long bench] as if all were waiting for someone. Servants wandering aimlessly around the courtyard hustled and soon after, Begum Mahmood alighted from inside the house in the presence of female relatives and servants. I don't remember any other scene as there were no light lamps after her arrival.[49]

She is also reported to have had a devastating wit as recounted by Scheherzade Tilat Alim, the great-granddaughter of Mahmood. One night, thieves broke into Musharraf Jahan's residence at Pili Kothi. On realising that they were preying on her safe on which she used to sit, she threw the keys at them and loudly cursed them. Hearing the commotion, the ladies of the house gathered and found her laughing uproariously. Seeing them perplexed by her reaction to the safe being stolen, Begum revealed that it was full of rocks and the thieves would definitely not be able to carry it.

In her old age, people called her *Gori Dadi* (fair granny), which was obviously due to her clear complexion. Hakim Syed Zillur Rahman, a Padma Shri awardee and former treasurer of AMU, in his book on Mahmood's son, Ross Masood, describes her as, 'Tall, rosy and fair, adorned with the dress of Old Delhi, a dupatta with a single thread of true *gota kanari* work, a *gharara*. The gathers of its skirt would have been so voluminous that one would have had to handle it with one hand.'[50]

The grave of Musharraf Jahan Begum is located in Sir Syed House, and on 26 January 2021, a rose garden was planted in her memory. On 1 April 2019, a 1500-bed residential hall for female students—the largest female residential hall at AMU—was christened in the memory of Mahmood's grandmother, Begum Azeezun Nisa.[51]

*Original building of Sir Syed House, which Mahmood gifted as dower to his wife, Musharraf Jahan Begum*

*Inauguration of Rose Garden in the memory of Syed Mahmood's wife, Musharraf Jahan Begum, on 26 January 2021, by Professor Tariq Mansoor, Vice Chancellor, AMU*

*Musharraf Jahan Rose Garden*

On 15 February 1889, Mahmood and Musharraf Jahan Begum were blessed with a boy, whom they named Ross Masood. The first name of the child was christened 'Ross', out of affection for Mahmood's very dear friend George E.A. Ross, a fellow barrister with whom Mahmood shared a house when he first moved to Allahabad as a judge. Reciprocating this very loving gesture, Ross and his wife adopted Ross Masood as their godson. Such was their bond that Mahmood's notebook contained his self-composed English poems dedicated to Ross and his wife.[52] Later on, after his appointment as a judge in the Allahabad High Court, he took leave from his onerous duties to visit his friend, who had settled in London.

Ross Masood had a very disciplined childhood, with Mahmood keeping a keen eye on his daily activities. Masood stayed with his mother at Pili Kothi in the MAO College campus at Aligarh while his father was serving as the high court judge in Allahabad.

*Sir Ross Masood, son of Syed Mahmood*

Mahmood's excessive drinking and consequent sensory disturbances marred their marital relations in the later years and also had a bearing on Masood's upbringing. Evidence of this is seen in the correspondence between Musharraf Jahan Begum and E.A. Molony, the then magistrate of Aligarh, which is also cited by other scholars, such as Alan M. Guenther. Molony's letter[53] testifies to Mahmood's overindulgence in alcohol leading to loss of health, violent temper, wavering sanity and deteriorating family affairs.

Other reasons that precipitated the discord between the couple were Mahmood's opposition to let his wife take their son to live with her family in Delhi and her parents' disapproval of English education. Some of Mahmood's apparently odd ways in the upbringing of their son, such as subjecting him to strenuous tasks of ploughing the soil on cold nights and forcing him to consume raw meat, were unacceptable to Musharraf Jahan Begum. On his part, Mahmood justified it by contending that since India is a predominantly agrarian economy, every Indian ought to know about agricultural practices. Regarding the consumption of raw meat, he contended, bemusingly so, that it would make Masood a 'lion cub.'[54]

She wrote a letter[53] to E.A. Molony, seeking the government's intervention to rescue her son by placing him under the guardianship of Theodore Morison,[55] requesting instructions for non-interference by Mahmood and the payment of maintenance from Mahmood in recovery of the debt he owed her.

After the demise of Mahmood in 1903, the then principal of MAO College, Theodore Morison, undertook the responsibility of 14-year-old Masood's education. His family took special interest in Masood, and under their care, he blossomed into a diligent young man. In 1905, he passed the matriculation examination and secured a government scholarship for higher education in England. He not only performed admirably in his studies but was a sports enthusiast as well, having been appointed captain of the college's tennis and boxing teams. In a letter[56] addressed to Viqar-ul-Mulk, a close confidant of Sir Syed, Theodore Morrison wrote about the progress of Ross Masood:

> You will, I am sure, be glad to hear how well Ross Masood has been doing in England. He has worked steadily and well at Oxford, and got his degree this year—taking a second in history which is considered a good class, if he cared to go in, he might just be in the Civil Service, but he does not wish to try. He has made excellent friends at Oxford, and all the best men in his college, in fact, and when I saw him among them it was obvious that Masood was a person of weight and influence in the College Society. Masood has also grown into a very fine, muscular young man, and he is now quite an athlete. He played tennis for his college and is now a fine player. His physical condition is proof of his excellent moral character.[57]

Masood earned Bachelor's in Arts Honours in 1910 from the Oxford University. Thereafter, following his father's footsteps, he joined the Lincoln's Inn. After completing his legal education in 1912, he returned to India and started his law practice at Patna. Alongside, he was elected as a trustee of MAO College on 13 January 1913.[58]

Masood rose to prominence after becoming the vice chancellor of AMU (1929–1934). He is credited for having revolutionised the academic atmosphere of AMU by introducing various new courses, establishing science laboratories and appointing foreign scholars of eminence. After tendering his resignation as vice-chancellor, he served as the education minister of Bhopal at the request of his friend and the then ruler of Bhopal, Nawab Hamidullah Khan. Masood was one of the founders of the Osmania University, Hyderabad. In 1933, the British government conferred upon him knighthood for his seminal contribution in the field of education. Masood also served as the president of *Anjuman Taraqqi-Urdu*[59]—an organisation working across India for the promotion of Urdu language. In 2011, it published the biography of Sir Ross Masood.

Masood was an affable personality, and his company was immensely cherished by his friends. Well-known poet–philosopher Mohammad Allama Iqbal and British novelist E.M. Forster were amongst his closest friends. Forster dedicated his famous novel *A Passage to India*, published in 1924, to Masood.

Syed Mahmood's life in law and education, as the subsequent chapters strive to show, was remarkable for the times he lived in—the time when the British Raj marginalised the 'native intelligentsia'. The son could achieve more as the environment was a little more enabling in the post-World War I period with the introduction of limited diarchy under the Government of India Act, 1919. In a way, Mahmood and Masood, taken as a father and son continuum, demonstrate a continuing thread of excellence. Both left their indelible marks as public intellectuals—though Mahmood arguably outshines the son in providing flesh and blood to the skeleton of the emerging Indian statutory laws through his thoughtful interpretation of the letter of law.

2

# Educationist: Contribution to the Aligarh Muslim University

Seldom does one try to locate Syed Mahmood beyond his much-acclaimed legal eloquence and judicial dexterity reflected in his judgments, and hence, his serious and groundbreaking engagements with other domains of knowledge have remained largely invisible. Not many know what Mahmood did after returning to India. On his return from England, he found Indians, especially Muslims, reeling in the quagmire of ignorance and it prompted him to make the propagation of education a means of eradicating all the ills engulfing them as priority. How he strove to shape the destiny of his fellow citizens through education needs to be told candidly before turning attention to his legal wizardry.

The establishment of MAO College—which later metamorphosed into AMU—in 1877 marks an epoch moment in the educational and social history of modern India. Its inception is considered the first significant response by the Indian Muslims to the challenges of the post-1857 era. This was an important catalyst in the process of social change, which allowed them to unshackle from medieval thinking towards broad-mindedness, reason, modernity and progress. The noted orientalist Sir Hamilton Gibb characterised it as 'the first modernist institution in Islam.'[1] The establishment of the college fostered among Indian Muslims an educational renaissance tethered to the aim of instilling an enlightened outlook towards religion and empowering them to make a mark in the emerging frontiers of knowledge.

## Constructing Mahmood's Grand Role

Syed Mahmood's contribution in the making of MAO College is pre-eminent. He dedicated his soul to the institution of his father's dreams. Although the institution started as the MAO 'college', in the vision and scheme of Mahmood, it was always a 'university' ab initio. A noted Urdu poet, Sheikh Mumtaz Husain Jaunpuri, wrote, 'The Aligarh Muslim University [sic] should be seen as the creation of Syed Mahmood's visionary scheme.'[2]

Sir Syed had great confidence in his son Mahmood and believed that none other than him could ensure the continuation of his vision for MAO College. He desired that Mahmood should succeed him, and therefore got him appointed as the honorary joint secretary of MAO College in 1887. In furtherance of his objective—later in 1889—on Sir Syed's insistence, a provision nominating Justice Mahmood to serve the Office of the Life Honorary Secretary, MAO College after the former's death was included.[3] Sir Syed paid glowing tributes to Mahmood for his contribution in the making of MAO College in the following words: 'Mahmood had typified in his person the spirit of MAO College.'[4]

## *Deconstructing the 'Muhammadan-Anglo' in MAO*

Sir Syed was always impressed by English education, and not surprisingly, it reflected in his vision for MAO College too. In 1882, in his testimony before the Hunter Education Commission,[5] he said that the purpose of MAO College was 'to form a class of persons, Muhammadan in religion, Indian in blood and colour, but English in tastes, in opinions, and in intellect'.[6]

However, David Lelyveld, arguably the most renowned scholar on the Aligarh Movement,[7] makes an interesting analysis of the context of this quote while advising caution in taking it at its face value. As Sir Syed had limited knowledge of English, Lelyveld accords high probability that it may have actually come from Syed Mahmood in the same way as several other English texts prepared by him in his father's name. Syed Mahmood had the benefit of English, which his father lacked. Instances of the son aiding his father in this have been well-documented.

Out of all such texts, the first is the booklet *Shortcomings of the Present Education System in India* prepared by Sir Syed with Mahmood's help, in which he made an effort to highlight the shortcomings of the educational system introduced in India by the British.[8] The second is a pamphlet authored by Mahmood but published in Sir Syed's name, in which an investigation was undertaken of the causes that prevented Muslims from availing themselves adequately of the government educational facilities, and to provide means by which they might be reconciled to the study of western arts and sciences.[9] The third text is the one where Mahmood was instrumental in reproducing Sir Syed's book on the prophet, *Khutbat-e-Ahmadiya*, in English. The most decisive evidence, however, is the episode of Sir Syed's resignation from the Hunter Commission—he faced considerable difficulty in pursuing the proceedings of the commission as he was not well versed in the English language.[10]

Based on this, Lelyveld concludes that the testimony of Sir Syed before the Hunter Education Commission—wherein he outlined the purpose of MAO College 'to form a class of persons, Muhammadan in religion, Indian in blood and colour, but English in tastes, in opinions, and in intellect'—is not an adequate description of the Aligarh Movement. Moreover, he is even unwilling to accept that it reflects the convictions of Syed Mahmood himself. Lelyveld is inclined to accept it as something rooted in a specific context and pragmatism in order to garner support of the British government for the nascent MAO College, and also for preferential treatment on some personal matters. He goes on to the extent of saying that 'such words don't necessarily reveal the full, inner heart for all the time of the people who say them.'[11]

Lelyveld has also probed the use of the word 'Anglo' and its hyphenation in 'Muhammadan Anglo-Oriental College'. This expression, according to him, is deeply relevant for understanding the mission of Sir Syed and his son in relation to the Muslim public they sought to mobilise, the colonial regime they tried to placate and the dynamics of their interpersonal relationship as father and son.

The Muhammadan Anglo-Oriental College was culminated into AMU by an Act of the Legislative Council of India in 1920. The notification of the *Gazette of India* was issued on 1 December 1920, though the formal ceremony of the university was held on 17 December 1920. Unfortunately, neither Sir Syed nor Syed Mahmood lived long enough to see the historic day. But the father–son duo had put together what was required to bring into existence the nucleus of an organisation which blossomed into a full-fledged modern university.

*Preparing a Blueprint for the University*

Sir Syed stayed in England for 17 months (1869 to 1870) and Mahmood rendered him his valuable assistance—from attending meetings with the British nobility to translating texts, as the former was not fully conversant with the lingua franca, that is, English. Sir Syed himself confessed that without Mahmood's help, his visit to England would have been a failure. Nobody knew of Sir Syed's plans more accurately than Syed Mahmood, who was a true replica of his father.[12]

The plan for MAO College was the outcome of prolonged discussions between them which included the details of the infrastructure, selection of the city and sketches of the college quadrangle—the magnificent Sir Syed Hall. In fact, even the detailed sketches of the college were jointly prepared by them with the help of British architects.[13]

*MAO College quadrangle, which Mahmood designed with the help of British architects*

David Lelyveld records Mahmood's assistance to his father:

> After seventeen months of living all together in a London flat engaged in intensive study, with occasional forays to ceremonial occasions as his father's translator, Syed Mahmood was finally left on his own to go up to Cambridge while simultaneously qualifying as a Barrister at Lincoln's Inn. During this period, however, he remained deeply engaged in his father's work, writing essays for *Tahzib ul-Akhlaq*, and preparing a lengthy and detailed plan for the educational establishment that his father planned to create at Aligarh. What his father expected of him was to master English culture in order to serve the Muslim cause.[14]

*Mecklenberg House—Syed Mahmood and his father's residence in London*

During his stay in England, Sir Syed desired to elicit the opinion of Indian Muslims on modern education in order to determine: Why modern education had not made much headway amongst them? What could be the possible causes of their disregard of Western culture? What steps should be taken to remove the impediments?

The appeal for inviting their opinions was drafted by Syed Mahmood with the help of his teachers.[13]

At the age of 22, Mahmood prepared a scheme in Urdu titled *Yuniwirsity Kaimbirij* (University of Cambridge), proposing an educational institution patterned on the lines of Cambridge University, but tailored to suit the peculiar needs of India. It was in the form of an essay that he sent to his father, which was later published in the *Aligarh Institute Gazette*.[15] This essay would later go on to form an integral part of the scheme[16] prepared by the *Kamiti–yi-Taraaqqi-yi-Ta'lim-i-Musalman*[17] (Committee for the Progress of Muslim Education) for MAO College.

In the essay, he described the establishment of the university and its colleges, administrative structure including masters and fellows, the daily-life activities of a student, and the various courses and examinations offered. The university allotted to each student two rooms—one as a bedroom and one for study and receiving friends. The prevalent custom among the students to fasten the outer door of their rooms to indicate that they were not in their rooms or that they did not wish to be disturbed in their studies also finds mention in his essay. His essay concluded with a suggestion for the committee to establish a school modelled after Cambridge.

On 26 December 1870, a committee *Kamiti–yi-Taraaqqi-yi-Ta'lim-i-Musalman* was constituted by Sir Syed, and he called upon Mahmood, who was then at Cambridge, to draft its constitution. This committee was entrusted with the task of drafting a scheme on the basis of the public opinion of Muslims about the need for modern education. Mahmood prepared a questionnaire which was sent to all the stakeholders for their opinion. Later, on 15 April 1872, this committee was renamed the 'MAO College Fund Committee'.

Syed Mahmood prepared an enterprising revised scheme[18] in 1873 for establishing an educational institution at Aligarh. This scheme holds the answer to how he planned to conjugate the expression 'Anglo' with 'Muhammadan'. The model he proposed was of a university, as distinguished from a school, marked by a cosmopolitan spirit in languages and encouraged advanced research in humanities. While it was inspired by the reforms proposed at Cambridge then, simultaneously, it was also designed to cater to the special needs and interests of the Muslims. It had the term 'university' for English and *Dar-ul-Uloom* for Urdu. This was adopted by the MAO College Fund Committee. In Mahmood's view, the committee's name should have had the word 'university' in place of 'college', and in Urdu it should have been called '*Dar-ul-Uloom*' instead of '*Madarsat-ul-Uloom*'; moreover, except for general supervision, the government should not have had any kind of interference in it.[19]

He further said in a meeting of the Fund Committee:

> The Committee calls itself as the M.A.O. College Fund Committee . . . I think what we mean is not a college but the University and I hope that the members will give effect to this resolution of February 1873 and instead of word 'College', the word 'University' may be substituted.[20]

The scheme stands out for its comprehensiveness and deserves elaboration. To begin with, it proposed the establishment of two separate institutions—a school and a college, integrated into a university. The preamble enlisted six conditions—applicable to both the school and college—aimed at building an institutional framework for its management, covering functional autonomy, financial autonomy, intellectual enlightenment, employability, fellowships and residential character. They read as below:

1) That the management of this institution should be perfectly *free from any control of the government* beyond mere supervision.

2) The university should secure for itself sufficient annual income to keep it *independent of any external aid*.
3) That the subject which is not exactly of any practical importance but which *improve the mind* should also be taught.
4) That the success in the course of study appointed by the University should bring with it *pecuniary advantage* to the students.
5) That at the end of a successful course study *emoluments* should be offered to successful students without any special duties attached to them.
6) The *residence* within the precincts of the University and under its discipline should be as indispensable as education in the course of study itself.[21] [emphasis added]

Stressing on their salience, he wrote:

> The above mentioned six conditions I consider to be great importance to any educational institution particularly to any University in India. I am so convinced that I can without hesitation say that unless they are adopted any attempt towards real education and enlightenment of my country must be a failure.[22]

On the first two conditions of autonomy, Mahmood argued that functional and financial autonomy are necessary as the British government—which 'is almost wholly . . . different from us in language, in religion and in mode of thought'—would not be able to fully understand our wants with respect to education. He supported his argument by stating that the best educational institutions in Europe are either entirely, or nearly, free from government control, even where rulers belong to the nation whose education is to be conducted. For attaining financial autonomy, he envisioned a model of internal endowment without external (government) aid.[23] This was indeed an audacious suggestion for proposing to keep the Crown at bay.

On the third condition for attainment of intellectual enlightenment of students, Mahmood delineated the role of education in igniting the minds. He professed that any education that does not enlighten the thought process of students, but merely capacitates their practical training, is of no greater use to the community than those who never go through the course of the university. The university should advance progressive ideas informed by sound and deep knowledge.

Mahmood included the fourth and fifth conditions, related to pecuniary advantages and institution of fellowships, based on his experiences at Cambridge and practices in European universities. He wrote:

> I have only to say pecuniary rewards are a great encouragement to study, even in the most civilised countries of Europe, and in India, where wealth and intellectual exertion seldom go together, they are more than encouragement. It often happens that those who wish to learn most have least to maintain themselves, and in such a case, pecuniary emoluments cannot fail to produce a good scholar.[24]

The sixth point of Mahmood's scheme for MAO College dealt with the residential character of the university, which he considered as indispensable as education in the course of study itself. He believed that this would encourage a strong bonding between the students and teachers. The higher objective behind the establishment of a university with a vast residential character was not merely to disseminate knowledge but to provide the necessary skills and mental attitude to face the vagaries of life. He wrote:

> Sixth point is of the most vital importance. It is to be the chief distinctive feature between our own institution and the Universities which already exist in India. The mode of life amongst the Musalmans of India requires far greater reform than even their mode of education. And unless we bring a large number of students and able teachers together in one place and form a society of Indian Muslamans, no educational project can be carried out to the considerable extent. The government educational institutions have lost a great deal of their utility on account of difficulty of introducing any change in life of their student and our University can do no better if residence of students within the precincts is not enforced.[25]

The first part of the scheme proposed the creation of a residential school as a preparatory institution for those who aspired to join the university. As a feeder institution, its object was to prepare a certain number of students who could successfully pursue the course of the university. For this, at the end of a five-year course at the school, an entrance test was proposed to be conducted for admission to the university. The Fund Committee resolved to establish similar schools in other towns wherever possible to prepare students for the university at Aligarh.

Thus, the first goal was to establish a school based on Cambridge's educational system. In a meeting on 10 February 1873, Mahmood observed that the school should be established under the patronage of *Madarsat-ul-Uloom* (a college) as soon as possible. In another meeting of the sub-committee on 31 August 1873, he reiterated his demand and finally it was decided that on 21 May 1875, coinciding with the birth date of the Queen, the school would be established.

The second part of the scheme dedicated to the college laid out the curriculum and pedagogy. The college was split into two departments—the lower vertical with four-year courses in general branches of knowledge for grounding in liberal education and the upper vertical with two-year courses for advanced knowledge in a specialised branch.

An eye-catching clause was the focus on music and languages besides the general subjects of study, as students had the option to choose from an array of languages—Arabic, English, Sanskrit, Latin and Greek. Another highlight was a provision for any person to join the university for the study of some special subject without an intention to pursue the full course of study. To foster research in all disciplines, 30 residential fellowships with an annual grant of ₹600 for a period of seven years were instituted.

*Nurturing the Nascent College*

Besides being an architect of the scheme plan, Mahmood invested his personal resources in translating the plan into action in its nascent stages. So, when it was decided that the college would be established in Aligarh, he purchased a bungalow there worth approximately ₹6,000 for his father and got it fitted in European style as Syed Ahmad had mortgaged their previous residence to Moulvi Samiullah Khan[26] before leaving for England.

Mahmood was in the headlines of newspapers on 8 January 1877 for delivering a passionate inaugural address at the foundation stone laying ceremony of MAO College. The address was a statement of his vision underpinning the scheme. Blending his oratory with prolific scholarship, it earned him accolades from Lady and Lord Lytton. Speaking on the autonomous character of the college, he said:

> There have been schools and colleges founded and endowed by private individuals. There have been others built by the sovereigns and supported by the revenue of the State. But this one is first time in the history of the Mohammedans of India that a college owes its establishment not to the charity or love of learning of an individual, not to the splendid patronage of a monarch, but to the combined wishes and united efforts of the community. It has its origins in the causes which the history of this country has never witnessed before. It is based upon principles of toleration and progress such as find no parallel in the annals of the East . . . .[27]

*Foundation stone–laying ceremony of MAO College*

*Foundation stone of MAO College*

Underlining his case for ingraining Western knowledge in oriental learning, so as to engender holistic education, he said:

> . . . to make these facts clear to the mind of our countrymen, to educate them so that they may be

> able to appreciate these blessings; to dispel those illusory traditions of the past which have hindered our progress; to remove those prejudices which have hitherto exercised a baneful influence on our race; to reconcile oriental learning with western literature and science, to inspire in the dreamy minds of the people of the east the practical energy which belongs to those in the West.[28]

Philosophising on the potential of the college to transform lives amongst Indians, he continued:

> [T]he seed which we sow today there may spring up a mighty tree, whose branches, like those of the banyan of the soil, shall in turn strike firm roots into the earth, and themselves send forth new and vigorous saplings; that this college may expand into a university, whose sons shall go forth throughout the length and breadth of the land to preach the gospel of free enquiry, of large hearted toleration, and pure morality.[29]

Most certainly, the seed sowed on the day, etched in Mahmood's enterprising scheme document, has turned into a mighty banyan tree, and deserves a contemporary retelling. A case in point is the residential character of AMU today, with most of the staff and students residing on campus. Its 19 halls of residence comprising 100 hostels cater to its 38,000 students, drawn from India's 36 states and union territories, 26 foreign countries, representing all religions, regions and languages of the country. Living on the same campus, dining on the same tables, playing on the same grounds and sharing together the joys and concerns of residential life has engendered an ecosystem of harmonious corporate living and has contributed to broad-mindedness at the university.

Speaking at the programme of the centenary celebrations of the university on 22 December 2020, Prime Minister Narendra Modi labelled AMU as a 'mini India'. By doing so, he portrayed the university as a microcosm of Indian society and a unique symbol of India's composite culture—where for centuries, despite many diversities, we are living as a people in unity and oneness.[30]

The prime minister said:

> One can see a mini India here that comprises several departments, dozens of hostels, thousands of teachers, and lakhs of students. AMU teaches Urdu on one side and Hindi on the other. Also, Arabic is taught, so is Sanskrit education. Here, the library has copies of the Quran and the translations of the Gita and Ramayana have been preserved with the same care. Diversity is not only a prestigious trait of AMU, but also the strength of the country. We must not forget this power, nor allow it to weaken it. The spirit of one India—superior India on the AMU campus keeps getting stronger day by day, we have to work together for this . . . .[31]

*Prime Minister Narendra Modi releasing the Special Commemorative Postal Stamp at the Centenary Celebration Programme of AMU on 22 December 2020*

*Centenary Gate—Centenary Commemorative Gate of AMU, 2020*

Another distinguishing element of the scheme has been the germination of school system within the university ecosystem. Today, AMU runs 10 schools, including four for girls and one for the visually challenged, with 15,000 students and 500 teachers feeding the university courses. This makes AMU one of the rare universities that offer education from primary to post-doctoral level.

Mahmood's conviction that the primary objective of education is to impart 'enlightened education' and not simply 'practical education', as outlined in the third condition of his scheme, resonates with the National Education Policy of 2020. The word 'enlighten' appears at four places in the text of the NEP 2020 to lend context to the ideals of 'knowledge society', 'quality higher education system', 'national progress' and 'indigenous problem solving'. They read as:

> . . . A quality higher education must enable personal accomplishment and *enlightenment* . . .[32]
>
> At the societal level, higher education must enable the development of an *enlightened*, socially conscious, knowledgeable, and skilled nation that can find and implement robust solutions to its own problems. . .[33]
>
> 'Research in the arts and humanities, along with innovation in the sciences and social sciences, are, therefore, extremely important for the progress and enlightened nature of a nation.[34]
>
> . . . research and knowledge creation . . . needs to be further strengthened to make India lead research and innovation in the twenty-first century, as a strong and *enlightened* knowledge society . . .[35] [emphasis added]

Mahmood's attention to minute details in modelling MAO College is striking—from architecture to uniform, boarding houses to reading rooms, traditions to literary discourse and debating—nothing could skip his meticulous eye.

He played a significant role in shaping the sociocultural life at MAO College and is credited for instilling the tradition of love for juniors and respect for seniors at the campus. He often recited verses in the company of his friends or before an informal audience. He is said to have recited extracts from Macaulay's *Horatius* and Hood's *Bridge of Sighs* at a meeting of the 'Penny Reading' in 1885, which was organised by the Siddons Club. Also known as Siddons Union or Siddons Union Club, it came into existence in 1884 at MAO College and was named after the first principal of the college, Henry George Impey Siddons. A debating hall called the Siddons Debating Union Hall was constructed on campus which consisted of a debating hall, a library and a reading room. Siddons Club was formally inaugurated in August 1884. Its membership was optional, with an annual fee of ₹9. The principal of the college was its ex officio president. The vice president and the secretary were elected for the session, the treasurer once in two years, while the members of the select committee were elected for a term of six months. Debates were held every Wednesday morning, thrice a month in English and once a month in Urdu. The hall maintained the library and the reading room and conducted meetings of the 'Penny Reading' once in two or three months.

The first debate of the club was held on 15 November 1884 on the topic 'The spread of female education is to be desired but by home tuition and not through schools and colleges'. The first meeting of the 'Penny Reading' was organised by the club on 5 September 1885 to which non-members from the city were admitted on payment of ₹2 each. The audience was entertained with the recitations from classics and works of well-known authors. In all, eight persons, including Mahmood, gave recitations on the occasion. The club thus became a centre of cultural and literary activities for Aligarh as a whole.[36]

It was Syed Mahmood's interest in the club's establishment and activities that made it the cultural hub at MAO College; the club's activities involved hosting a variety of audiences and organising various literary events at the campus. He also established a Persian society at Aligarh, which was instrumental in stimulating interest in Persian poetry and literature. In 1880, in line with Cambridge boarding houses, he established a reading room at MAO College. Interestingly, he even got the gowns for the students designed similar to the one he wore as a Cambridge student. He further proposed the composition of the governing body of the college similar to that at Cambridge.

He passionately taught English at MAO College and took personal interest in the affairs of the college at Aligarh, despite his pressing commitments as a high court judge at Allahabad. Important administrative and academic tasks of the college were overseen by him. Moreover, he participated in the selection process of the staff and liaised with the director of public instruction and other government authorities on behalf of Sir Syed. Most letters and communications were drafted by him.

In 1883, he took a leave without pay from his work and went to England to recruit a headmaster for MAO College from Cambridge University. He returned with Theodore Beck from Cambridge, whom he recruited with the assistance of Arthur Strachey, son of Sir John Strachey, an ardent supporter of Sir Syed since the 1857 revolt. Inspired by his charisma, Beck agreed to model MAO on the patterns of Cambridge. He travelled back to India along with Syed Mahmood after being vigorously oriented and inducted into the philosophy of the Aligarh Movement by Mahmood.

*Theodore Beck, who was recruited by Syed Mahmood as principal of MAO College*

On 2 September 1899, Principal Theodore Beck died in Shimla. Professor Theodore Morison, a graduate from Trinity College, Cambridge, who joined MAO College as a professor of English the same year, was appointed the principal on 29 October 1899. He had the following words of commendation for Mahmood's efforts in nurturing the college in its early years:

> The debt which the College owed in early years to the late Mr. Syed Mahmood cannot be overestimated, the generous help which he gave it from his private purse has never been made public and he, even more than his father, was responsible for the original design of a residential College for Muhammadans, though the credit of the far harder task of putting the plan into practice is solely due to the dauntless courage and pertinacity of Sir Syed . . . .[37]

Mahmood affirmed his foremost and lifelong commitment towards the educational objectives underlining the Aligarh Movement and MAO College, even at the cost of his other commitments. In one of his letters towards the end of his judgeship, he wrote:

> So far as my own personal feelings in regard to my father's life long work are concerned, I have long ago given him my word of honour that upon his [Sir Syed] death I shall put aside everything which would be inconsistent with employing my best energies in carrying on the work to which he has devoted the greatest and best portion of his life

namely the amelioration of the educational and socio-political condition of the Mohammedans by promoting in them intellectual and moral enlightenment and feeling of deep and real loyalty towards the British Rule in India. He is now about 76 years of age, and though usually enjoying fair health has so often given apprehensions to his friends and admirers among the Trustees of the College that so long ago of the 28th December 1889, and again on the 30th December 1892 they passed Rules and Regulations of the College in the form of a Code in which they devote a chapter to Rules regarding my father and myself personally to secure my succession to him by appointing me the first Life Honorary Joint Secretary, and even during my father's life entrusting me with almost plenary powers in matters connected with position, rights and privileges of the European Officers of the College—the European Instructive Staff consisting of a Principal, three Professors and a Head Master.[38]

*Enquiry in the Embezzlement of 1895*

In July 1895, the trustees of the college, Syed Vilayat Hussain and Mirza Abid Ali Beg, discovered discrepancies in the MAO College Fund amounting to ₹1,07,198. Upon investigation, it was found that Shyam Bihari Lal, the head clerk of the college, had forged signatures of Sir Syed on cheques to withdraw the amount.

To recover the amount and the interest payable on it, criminal proceedings were initiated by Syed

Mahmood—who was the then honorary joint secretary of the college and had resigned from judgeship of the high court two years before and had subsequently joined the Bar. He made available his services to MAO College pro bono by conducting proceedings of criminal cases continuously for two months from 9 AM to 5 PM. He himself prepared the notes and explained and discussed all evidence with several barristers working with him.[39]

Although Shyam Bihari was convicted, the amount embezzled could not be recovered from him as it was much higher than the value of his property. He later committed suicide while in jail.

## Development of Legal Education at MAO College

The programme of legal education at the British universities had made an impression on Sir Syed Ahmad Khan during his visit to the country. Moreover, having seen the impact of legal education in shaping his son's intellect and personality, Sir Syed prioritised development of legal education at MAO College. So, when the college was established in 1877, the Department of Law became one of its initial units with its foundation laid on 1 January 1883.[40] Another reason for commencing legal education before starting other degree courses at the college was the desire to step up enrolment—as a major motive for English education among Indian Muslims was to improve self-employment prospects. Despite Sir Syed's initial interest in developing the law vertical at the college, the Department of Law in its early phases remained unknown to many, and its process of formalisation started only after Syed Mahmood drew his attention towards it in the later part of the decade.

Sir Syed constituted a committee comprising Justice Mahmood and Justice Straight (both of the Allahabad High Court) and Arthur Strachey, barrister-at-law (a practising lawyer at Allahabad) to suggest steps to be taken for the commencement of teaching of law at MAO College. The committee submitted a comprehensive scheme in March 1890, which culminated in the inauguration of law classes by Justice Douglas Straight on 29 December 1891 at the Scientific Society building (presently a part of the Ajmal Khan Tibbiya College at AMU).[41]

*Building where the law classes of MAO College commenced and where Syed Mahmood taught*

Initially meant to produce professional lawyers, the Department of Law was managed by legal practitioners and patronised by Syed Mahmood, who played a major role in its establishment and development. His personal imprint helped the department raise its standard, as most of the faculty members were appointed by a committee that had him as its member.

Mahmood ensured that only a man of dependable scholarship was appointed as the professor of law; after meticulous search, he appointed Barrister Syed Karamat Hussain as the first teacher, who also headed the department until 1891.[42] Syed Karamat Hussain later became a judge at the Allahabad High Court. With the efforts of Justice Karamat, the number of students at MAO College increased by 29 within a year, and many graduates qualified for various government services.

The pre-eminence accorded to the evolution of legal education at AMU, relative to other fields, is on two counts. First, the foundation of the department of law was laid down by AMU founder Sir Syed himself, and second, Sir Syed, too, was a 'man of law'.

In 1841, Sir Syed had been appointed as a munsif[43] in Mainpuri district of eastern Uttar Pradesh (UP). In later years, he served in higher positions of *Sadr Amin*[44] and *Sadr-us-Sudoor*[45] in various districts of UP and Delhi. In 1867, he was appointed as the judge of the small causes court in Banaras. His tenure there is known with reference to a case for non-payment of debt filed against Bhartendu Harishchandra (1850–1885), father of modern Hindi literature and theatre. Sir Syed settled the case by personally paying the amount due to the claimant.

In 1878, he was made a member of the viceroy's council, which was the central legislature of the time. The *Aligarh Institute Gazette* carried a piece welcoming his nomination to the council. It stated, 'Sir Syed will be found raising a manly voice in council; as far from popularity haunting and false patriotism on one side as from sycophancy and time serving on the other.'[46] His tenure is marked by interventions on causes having a bearing on the life of common man and alleviating their hardships. Besides piloting two key private bills—the Smallpox Vaccination Bill and Kazi Bill—he also put forth his views and drafted inputs on several others, notably the Transfer of Property Bill, the Wakf Bill, the Easement Bill, the Local Self Government Bill for Central Provinces, the Deccan Agriculturalists' Relief Act and the Ilbert Bill. Both private bills introduced by him were passed in 1880. The Smallpox Vaccination Bill mooted compulsory vaccination against a raging smallpox at the time that claimed thousands of lives of small children. The Kazi Bill led to the conferment of legal status on the *kazis*,[47] and acceptance of the long-pending demand of Muslims for resolution of personal disputes outside the formal court system.

As described earlier, because Sir Syed's knowledge of English was very limited, it is assumed that Syed Mahmood had assisted him in drafting his legislations in English, in the same way as he had done with his other works. In 2021, Professor Shafey Kidwai—a Sahitya

Akademi awardee and well-known scholar of the Aligarh Movement—in his book titled *Sir Syed Ahmad Khan: Reason, Religion and Nation*[48] has documented the legal contributions of Sir Syed.

Syed Mahmood had indeed inherited the legal acumen of his father, which was not only reflected in Mahmood's judicial acuity—as described in the later part of this book—but also in his dexterity as a legal educationist in shaping one of modern India's oldest legal education institution at AMU.

The Department of Law was included in the fleet of the first 15 departments when MAO college was upgraded to the status of 'university' in 1920. Over the years, the department has succeeded in carving a niche for itself as a premier institute of legal studies in India. It has since produced a number of luminaries who distinguished themselves in the bench, bar, academia, politics, etc.

### *Mahmood as a Law Teacher*

Often, Syed Mahmood himself engaged classes of English and law at MAO College. For law students, Mahmood intended to make legal studies a dual exercise—to attain occupational ambitions and pursue intellectual pleasure. He introduced the Socratic method of learning that promoted interactive learning and discussions to explore difficult legal concepts. He would himself formulate the test questions that required legal opinion on hypothetical cases, which gave students the opportunity to develop critical thinking and enabled them to approach law as intellectuals.

The *Legum Baccalaureus* (undergraduate law degree), which became a post-graduate degree in 1896, was awarded to 24 Aligarh students of the first generation. To the new college entrants, Mahmood would begin their orientation by telling them that since they were no longer boys, but 'gentlemen undergraduates', their responsibilities in matters of education were also greater. The ensuing point would be to fervently impress upon the class to *learn to think*. The phrase was spoken in a tone that resounded in the class, and it was repeated many times to drive home its importance.[49] A recollection of his classroom lecture by one of his students gives a detailed account of his unique teaching pedagogy. He started by posing a question to the students, and when answered even remotely to the point, he looked much pleased and exclaimed, 'Well done, my young friend, stand up that I may embrace you, your ability certainly has no bounds, you are a wonder, a prodigy, but take your seat, you have missed the point . . . .'[50]

After explaining his views on a topic, on the following day, he would make it a point to get the students to write their own views on what had been explained in the previous class. His conversations were always highly instructive. Whatever he spoke seemed to be a series of easy deductions from a single principle. He never led one to the thickest part of the subject before making him a master in its preliminary points. However strange and difficult be the subject, it was impossible for one to not understand what he tried to make them understand.[51] 'I had to compare the views of Austin[52], Rattigan[53] and Mahmood, and I was convinced that Mahmood's views were the clearest and the easiest to learn and remember,' recalled one of his students.[50]

As a legal scholar with a gifted sense of prescience, he naturally realised the importance of imparting legal education in a transdisciplinary fashion. He taught the principles of law with the help of analogies from arts and sciences more pleasing to the mind than law, underscoring that real knowledge lies at the point of intersection of many disciplines. For instance, on the concept of ownership, one of his students wrote a recollection in the *Aligarh Institute Gazette* as follows:

> As for example he often spoke of his having discovered that the right of ownership with its component rights was just like a masonry arch—graceful and complete—with the only difference that its key-stone was not like that of a mason's. A mason's key-stone, as soon as it was hammered down at the top fastened into one compact whole all otherwise separate pieces of stone in the arch. 'But my key-stone is in the arch of ownership is not like that, which is great pity. It breaks the analogy.'[50]

Mahmood also identified talent and persuaded students to take up law as a career option. Former Chief Justice of India M. Hidayatullah in his autobiography *My Own Boswell*, has acknowledged Justice Mahmood's contribution in shaping the career of the young students at MAO College. In reference to his father—Khan Bahadur Hafiz Mohammed Wilayatullah (*Kaiser-i-Hind*),[54] a student of MAO College—Justice Hidayatullah, wrote:

> Justice Mahmood, who had resigned from the Allahabad High Court in December 1893, persuaded

> him (my father) to take up Law. Justice Mahmood was always anxious to transmit his knowledge of law to a deserving student, and he chose my father on the strength of the latter's performance.[55]

Apart from MAO College, Mahmood also served as a fellow and member of Faculty of Law at the University of Calcutta, and fellow and president of Faculty of Law at the University of Allahabad in 1887.[56]

*Contributions to the Law Library*

Syed Mahmood practised educational philanthropy as a passion. To further the development of teaching–learning of law, he donated his own rare collection of books valued around ₹10,000 then to the law section in the MAO College library. He denied the proposal of Theodore Beck (principal of MAO College) to have the library so established to be named after him.

Sir Syed is known to have often relied on his son's meticulous advice even on routine matters related to the college. On one such instance, he received a letter from Mahmood dated 15 June 1893 containing detailed suggestions for drawing up a code of conduct for the MAO College library. The letter suggested, inter alia, the procedure for the issue and return of books, the class of persons eligible to use and borrow books, the duration for which the books could be borrowed, the limit on the number of books to be issued to a user, the creation and maintenance of an account register of each user, the audit of user-account register by designated authorities, the bar on the further lending of books by the borrowers, etc.

'No person who takes any books out of the Law Library under the preceding paragraphs should be authorised to lend those books to any person .... Audit by principal of the register maintained by the Librarian ...' read the extracts of the letter.[57]

The rules in the form of code of conduct as enumerated in the letter were accepted in their entirety and remarkably continue to this day.

Not only did he donate his valuable books, but he also offered to bear the cost of infrastructure required to store them. Fortunately, his books are still in the possession of the Department of Law. Several reports which are a part of this collection bear handwritten notes prepared by him for delivering lectures on various topics. He wrote:

> If the Trustees of the College accept my proposals, I will pay from my own pocket the cost of the almirah required for the law books to be put up in the Mehdi Manzil[58] and also the cost of other furniture such as tables, chairs and benches required for adapting the two rooms to convenient use-of the law library as above suggested by me.[57]

He also paid for the transit of books as evidenced by the *Aligarh Institute Gazette*. 'I will further pay such expense as you have incurred on behalf of the college in bringing the books from Allahabad to Aligarh,' he wrote further.[57]

The efforts of Syed Mahmood in nurturing the law faculty at MAO College was not confined to only producing legal practitioners but also to training budding legal minds to serve the nation as academics and judges. In the pursuit of this great vision, he made provisions for higher intellectual discourse. He wrote:

> That the two rooms of Mehdi Manzil furnished sufficient space for law professors or any other person allowed by the Trustee to deliver lectures on special branches of the higher departments of law, such as international law including the law of domicile, the rules of conflict of laws, the history of law and legal institutions, the interpretation of statutes and legal documents, and other similar subjects which are not usually compulsorily required either by the Indian Universities or other examining boards in India, may here be allowed to say that it is my own intention as soon as circumstances permit to deliver a series of lectures to selected students of the law class on some difficult and isolated questions of the higher departments of law which are not usually taught in the law classes of Indian colleges and are not included in the ordinary law examinations.[57]

For this reason, probably, the library at the Department of Law and some other departments of AMU is called 'seminar library'.

The consignment that contained the donated books also contained an imported hand-painted portrait of Justice Straight and a cheque of ₹1,000, which still adorns the Mehdi Manzil.

The noted Islamic law jurist Professor Tahir Mahmood recounts his student days spent at the AMU law faculty in his book *Reminiscing on Law Brains*. He wrote:

> On reaching Aligarh for my LLM studies I found in the gifts section of the Law Faculty library a large number of old and soiled books autographed by the donor. The attractive signatures seemingly put by old fashioned pens with nibs dipped in blue ink were a great inspiration for me. I kissed them, rubbed my eyes with them, and continued doing so frequently during my studies in the library.
>
> There were two reasons for my reverential attachment to those books. First, years earlier in 1920s some of these books must have been seen and read by my late father who was then an LLB student there. Second, the donor of these books was none else than one of the greatest judges of 19th Century India, AMU founder Sir Syed Ahmad Khan's illustrious son Justice Syed Mahmood.[59]

*Syed Mahmood Hostel—a hostel in the Sir Syed Hall of Residence for Boys, AMU, named after Syed Mahmood*

Syed Mahmood's tryst with education as outlined above stands apart in the way this first-generation English-educated person visualised blending the modern pedagogy with the intellectual heritage of his ancestors. This approach enabled him to evolve qualities of mind that made him taller than most of his compatriots in his vision of education and law as harbingers of social change, thereby building a more humane and enlightened India.

# 3

# Career in Law and as a Judge

From the foregoing chapter, it is evident that Syed Mahmood's fame in education had preceded his fame in law. For someone aged only 23 to have designed a full-fledged scheme for a university, which saw fruition only four years later, remains a feat in the annals of Indian educational history that has not been discoursed enough. It comes as rather surprising to observers of history that he chose law as a career instead of building on his already obvious talents as an educator. This was also at variance with what his father had planned and hoped from him. After Mahmood's return from England, Sir Syed wanted him to make a career in academia alongside continuing to assist him in his educational mission at Aligarh. In the *Aligarh Institute Gazette* of 18 July 1887, Sir Syed expressed his unfulfilled desire:

> If Syed Mahmud had not accepted a seat on the Bench of the High Court, and as he himself at different times thought (and I must say I was delighted at the idea) if he had come to the College, as a Professor, I would have entertained a higher respect for him and considered it a greater honour for himself and a source of much satisfaction to myself.[1]

Even though Mahmood himself did not elaborate on his closer embrace of law, several reasons may be attributed to it. To begin with, it was possibly an outcome of the influence that legal education in England had exerted on him. At a personal level, keeping in view Mahmood's independent nature, it offered him an avenue to come into his own by emerging out of his father's shadow. Another impetus might have been his convictions to leverage his training in law, in addition to education, as an instrument of positive social change. Certainly, his accomplishments as a judge, as this and the next chapter proves, enabled him to apply both. Whatever may have been the impetus for choosing law as his profession, he did concurrently remain devoted to his passion for the educational movement led by his father, albeit in a more subdued way.

## Initial Years in Legal Profession

After the quelling of the 1857 revolt, the colonial government undertook a series of measures for reforming and overhauling the judicial institutions. The passing of the Indian High Courts Act of 1861 by the British Parliament led to the establishment of high courts in the three presidency towns of Calcutta, Madras and Bombay. A provision in the Act conferred powers on the Crown to set up similar high courts in future in other territories of India. Consequently, a high court in Allahabad was established. The genesis for Allahabad High Court is found in a correspondence dated 24 June 1864, from the secretary of state for India to the governor general in council for creation of a high court for the North-Western Provinces.[2] Eighteen months later, on 17 March 1866, the High Court of Judicature for the North-Western Provinces was set up by a royal charter. Initially, the seat of the new high court was at Agra, until it was shifted to Allahabad in the year 1869 upon the completion of its building.

Syed Mahmood belongs to the first-generation lawyers to join the new high court in 1872 at Allahabad—practising before the High Court of the North-Western Provinces (now High Court of Judicature at Allahabad) as a qualified barrister. At the time, he was the lone non-European barrister in the region. During his initial years, Moulvi Samiullah Khan, an associate of his father at Allahabad, imparted him practical training of the profession. As a barrister from 1872 to 1878, he appeared before the courts in Punjab, central provinces and Awadh, arguing matters pertaining to Muslim personal law, general civil law and criminal law. His initial practice is not known to be successful and reportedly did not attract many clients. To sustain his living in Allahabad, he accepted an offer of appointment to teach law as a sub-professor at the Muir Central College, Allahabad.

In 1876, at the age of 26, Mahmood translated into Urdu the Indian Evidence Act, 1872 and wrote a commentary on, *Sharahe-Qanun Shahadat Majria Hind*, the same in Hindustani. He is believed to have ventured into this task with the objective of enlightening law practitioners and trial court judges about the rules of evidence in a language well known to them. He understood that although the Indian Evidence Act is relevant in all cases and in all courts, its need is greatest in the trial courts. Often the high court, the Privy Council and the advocates practising there expressed concern that there was either a deficiency in bringing on record the right material for disposal of the case, or irrelevant material was brought on record, or sometimes good evidence was left out.

Mahmood's book sought to fill this gap and lucidly explained the concept of 'law' and 'evidence'. It logically enumerated in detail the principles underlying the Indian Evidence Act, 1872. Notably, he refrained from giving his opinion on the controversial aspects and confined himself to the principles dealt by other distinguished authors, namely, Bentham, Taylor, Roscoe, Starkie, Norton, Goodeve and Cunningham. Various copies of this commentary were subsequently sold and published by the office of the secretary, MAO College. Mahmood dedicated the book to John Pearson—a practising barrister at Lincoln's Inn in London who gave Mahmood early training of the profession in England.

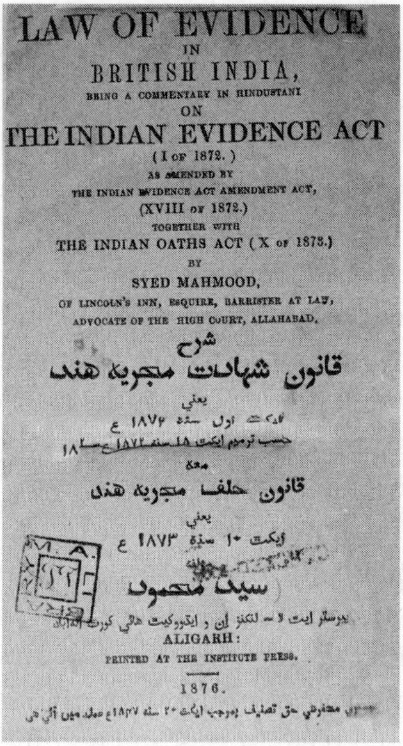

LAW OF EVIDENCE
IN
BRITISH INDIA,
BEING A COMMENTARY IN HINDUSTANI
ON
THE INDIAN EVIDENCE ACT
( I OF 1872. )
AS AMENDED BY
THE INDIAN EVIDENCE ACT AMENDMENT ACT,
(XVIII OF 1872.)
TOGETHER WITH
THE INDIAN OATHS ACT ( X OF 1873.)
BY
SYED MAHMOOD,
OF LINCOLN'S INN, ESQUIRE, BARRISTER AT LAW,
ADVOCATE OF THE HIGH COURT, ALLAHABAD.

شرح
قانون شهادت مجریه هند
یعني
معه
قانون حلف مجریه هند
یعني
سید محمود

ALIGARH:
PRINTED AT THE INSTITUTE PRESS.
1876.

*Syed Mahmood's commentary on the Indian Evidence Act, 1872*

## Appointment as a Judge

In July 1879, Mahmood joined the Civil Services as a district judge (third grade). Lord Lytton, the then viceroy of India, commissioned him as the district and sessions judge of Raebareli on 1 August 1879.

It is interesting to note that contemporaneous with his recruitment to the civil services, he laboured for greater affinity with the colonial government in varied forms. A striking reference is the article he wrote for the *Calcutta Law Review* in 1879 for the British audience, supposedly for investigating the nature and causes of friction in relations between the English and Indians.[3] The article has been largely interpreted by historians as being apologetic to the British, which is somewhat contrary to Mahmood's claims of it being an honest and impartial rendering of the defects and shortcomings of British rule in India. In Mahmood's reading of the causes that are detrimental to the stability of British rule, he advocated for 'liberal imperialism' in India, according to which the continuation of British rule was necessary for order and good governance of the country, but it was being compromised by their antagonistic conduct.[4] The following extract in the introductory part of the article is conspicuous:

> I am inspired with all loyalty and due from a subject of a peaceful State towards a rule the security of which I, in common with millions, look upon as an absolute necessity of order and good government of this country, as [the] only means [of] her future prosperity and civilisation. I look upon British rule for India as the only alternative of anarchy and barbarism.[5]

On the origin of British rule in India, Mahmood contentiously argued that the British rule in India was founded on consent and cooperation and not on physical force. His reading in international law led him to contest the then prevalent notion that the British had acquired India by conquest. He wrote:

> The word *conquest* is a term in international law and has a definite meaning. It means the acquisition of territorial dominion by open force. The greater

> portion of British dominions in India was not acquired by open force—it was acquired by means far different from physical violence. Some of the provinces now under the Viceroy of India were acquired without the expenditure of a single drop of blood. If conquest presupposes war, India cannot be said to have been conquered in the sense in which the word ought to be legitimately understood. The first footing of East India Company in Bengal was not the result of brute force or military violence. Rather, the company began by being peaceful traders, subject to laws which, at that time, governed the province of Bengal. Their commerce flourished; their rights were not sufficiently respected; and by force of necessity, rather than by intention of conquest, they took steps which gave them sovereignty of Bengal and ultimately of India.[6]

A section of the present-day scholarship on colonialism considers the theory that Indians consented to be colonised as part of a rhetoric devised by the Raj itself to justify their conquest, and played along by apologetics, most notably, John R. Seeley in his book *The Expansion of England*. Interestingly, Jon Wilson, a professor of modern history at King's College, London, notes that Seeley probably knew Mahmood from his Cambridge days—with the former serving as a faculty member at the time the latter was a student at the same college. Wilson suggests that Seeley's book was premised on the arguments of Mahmood's article. The similarity of the line of argument leads Wilson to imply that either the two had had a conversation on the subject during their time together, or Seeley plagiarised the proposition from Mahmood's lectures.[7]

However, it is somewhat problematic to imply that Mahmood's views in his article are an accurate reflection of his convictions about the Raj. The more plausible explanation is that given the larger socio-political scenario of the time, Mahmood's defense of the Raj, albeit wrapped in academic sophistry, was driven by strategic personal objectives—for his own advancement in the civil services and to strengthen the political patronage of the government to the education institution he helped his father establish—rather than by conviction.

Later in 1881, Mahmood went on deputation to the state of Hyderabad, where he rendered legal advisory services to Sir Salar Jung, the then prime minister of Hyderabad, on a monthly salary of ₹2,000. He was made a member of the commission to suggest measures for legal and judicial reforms in the state, with the objective to simplify the laws of the state.[8]

On his return to northern India in November 1883, he rejoined as a district judge in Raebareli. As the district judge, his judgment in the case of *Deputy Commissioner Rae Bareli v. Rampal*[9] marked a turning point in his judicial career.

His legal acumen in interpreting the finer points governing the law of mortgages shone through the judgment. The judgment settled the issue *whether the terms of the deed entitled the mortgagee to sue for possession*. He interpreted the law to allow a *mortgage without possession* to be legally converted to a *mortgage with possession*, where the terms of the mortgage deed provided for such conversion.

In the instant case, the deed provided for such a conversion in case of default. Moreover, it stipulated that if the mortgagor defaulted on the amount of instalment due and objected to the application of rents accruing on the mortgaged property to be applied in payment of the debt, the mortgagee would be entitled to take immediate possession of the property mortgaged.

The decision was challenged before the Judicial Commissioner of Oudh William C. Capper who, through a judgment dated 31 October 1881, set aside the judgment of the district judge of Raebareli.

The deputy commissioner of Raebareli, the original plaintiff, moved an appeal before the Privy Council against the judgment of the judicial commissioner. The appeal was heard by Justice Fitzgerald, Justice B. Peacock, Justice R.P. Collier, Justice R. Couch and Justice A. Hobhouse. In the judgment dated November 1884, authored by Justice R. Couch for all Lordships, the Privy Council set aside the impugned decision and upheld the judgment given by Syed Mahmood. Extensively quoting verbatim the judgment authored by Syed Mahmood, the council observed:

> *What is said by the District Judge in his judgment is very pertinent to this part of the instrument*. The instrument must be looked at as a whole, and in their Lordships' opinion the reasonable construction is that there was an absolute power to the mortgagee to take possession on default in payment of an instalment, but if the mortgagor objected to the mortgagee applying

> the rents in reduction of the principal and interest, the mortgagee might sell the mortgaged property and other property which was brought into the security, in order to satisfy the debt. This seems to their Lordships to be the reasonable construction of the instrument. *It is the construction which the District Judge put upon it, but which the Judicial Commissioner thought was wrong, and therefore reversed his judgment. Their Lordships will humbly advise Her Majesty to reverse the decree of the Judicial Commissioner, leaving the judgment of the District Judge to stand.*[10] [emphasis added]

Mahmood's 46-page judgment, which includes 32 pages handwritten by him, is preserved in the museum of the Allahabad High Court. In 1973, the *Aligarh Law Journal* carried a detailed case comment on this judgment titled 'The Case that Raised Syed Mahmood to High Court Judgeship'.

The judgment earned him a strong recommendation for elevation to the high court. The members of the judicial committee of the Privy Council conveyed to the secretary of state for India, '. . . so talented a person should not be wasted in the subordinate judiciary.'[11]

On the extraordinary potential of Mahmood, George Farquhar Irving Graham, the author of *Life and Work of Syed Ahmed Khan*, wrote, 'I also told Syed Mahmud, when he came out from England in 1873, that he would be the first native judge in the High Court, NWP.'[12]

The then viceroy of India, Lord Lytton, was highly impressed with the articulation and oratory skills of Mahmood after hearing his passionate speech at the foundation stone laying ceremony of MAO

College in 1877. This impression had also played into his appointment as the district judge. Mahmood himself was aware of Lytton's intervention. In a letter addressed to Sir Richard Meade, a British Indian Army officer, Mahmood has acknowledged the fact that the personal interest of Lord Lytton paved the way for his appointment as the district judge.[13]

Lord Ripon, who succeeded Lord Lytton as the viceroy of India, actively lobbied for Mahmood's appointment as a permanent judge of the high court. In his letters addressed to the Marquis of Hartington, the secretary of state for India, he suggested the appointment of a native judge to the Allahabad High Court and recommended Mahmood's name for judgeship.[14]

It is also pertinent to remember the broader socio-political milieu of the time—one from which Mahmood benefitted. This was also the period in which the colonial government had started co-opting local notables in the higher judicial system. In the view of the government, the representation of local notables would, in the eyes of the native population, enhance the legitimacy of the colonial legal institutions and legal reforms initiated after the 1857 revolt, including the large-scale codification of laws. Back in 1869, the government allowed the natives to serve as judges of the high courts provided they had been called to the Bar in England. Mahmood's sound professional abilities and his conditioning to the English legal world and the Muslim world through the MAO project were considered ideal in the eyes of the government.

Mahmood first officiated as a temporary judge of the Allahabad High Court at the age of 32 in 1882,[15] and on three other occasions in 1884, 1886 and 1887. His temporary appointments were in place of judges who either went on furlough or had retired. His elevation as a temporary judge struck a welcome note at the time. *Indu Prakash*, an Anglo-Marathi periodical published in late 1880s and early 1900s, reported on 3 March 1884:

> The Allahabad High Court once more witnesses the accession of a native lawyer to its Bench in the nomination of Mr. Mahmood to act for Mr. Justice Tyrrel, who has gone on furlough. Mr. Justice Mahmood has sat more than once on the Allahabad Bench and his decisions, which are found in recent volumes of Law Reports of that Court, are written in a remarkably clear and vigorous style and show such a wide acquaintance with law that in the legal world he deservedly enjoys, we believe, the reputation of an able and conscientious Judge.[16]

On completion of each tenure as a temporary judge, he reverted to his substantive post as district judge. He was finally elevated as a permanent judge on 9 May 1887. By doing so, he made history by becoming the first Muslim and north Indian to be appointed to any high court under the British Empire in India, besides holding the distinction of being the youngest high court judge appointed till date. In fact, at the time, it was the highest rung of the judicial ladder in British India.

It is fascinating to note that even this rare patronage did not affect his judicial independence. One wonders if those who made him the judge were fully aware of the consequences. Mahmood, through his dissents, became a shredding machine of the colonial judicial convention of conformity with the British judges.

## Scholarly Judge

As a jurist and scholar of law, Justice Mahmood stood out for bringing his own insights into the law through the reading of original texts—a rare art in his times! Blessed with the hands and mind of an artist, he gave life to the black letters of law in his decisions.

Mahmood had the ability to succinctly manifest his entire judgment in two words, 'I concur', and immerse himself for months to write marvellous dissents that substantially contributed to the development of law in India. His pièce de résistance was acquaintance with seven languages that enabled him to master comparative jurisprudential scholarship.

He was known for adopting a liberal interpretation of law that furthered the principles of justice, equity and good conscience for resolution of disputes where the law was silent. Justice, equity and good conscience are legal rules employed to meet the necessity of doing what is right and fair, in situations where there is no suitable formal law for deciding a case. The rules are adopted by courts to secure justice, or to put it negatively, to present the miscarriage of justice. His liberal interpretations helped overcome the obstacles to resolve cases that fell in grey areas of law or where the law fell short of providing any specific rule to meet the circumstances of the case before it.

The decision delivered by Justice Mahmood in *Ishri v. Gopal Saran*[17] is a classic example wherein he invoked the principles of equity to adjudicate on a case where rules fell short. The judgment had the effect of entrenching the law on 'set-off' in India. Tracing the roots of the law of 'compensation' under the principles of equity, he identified a gap that this law was not fully developed in India or England.

Drawing on his deep knowledge of Roman jurisprudence, he borrowed the Roman law doctrine of *compensatio est debiti et crediti inter se contribution*. The doctrine is based on the concept of 'mutual contribution of debit and credit'. When two parties have a debt against each other of equal value, the rule of compensation or set-off provides a remedy in their common interest: to interchange a discharge of obligations—extinction of debts reciprocally due, effected by credits reciprocally held. It is for the convenience of parties that the law provides that the parties can mutually settle their amounts due to each other. Where the parties to a suit for recovery of money mutually own debts towards each other, the equitable doctrine of set-off provides that they can opt to settle the amount in one suit, thereby saving the parties from the hassle of a second suit.

The following extract captures the essence of the judgment:

> Is there, then, anything in the Code, or any equitable consideration which would prohibit a pre-emptor-decree-holder from availing himself of the doctrine

of set-off by deducting the costs allowed to him from the purchase-money which he has to deposit under the very decree which awards him costs? *The Civil Procedure Code, as we have pointed out, falls short of providing any specific rule to meet exactly the case before us.* The doctrine of set-off, which owes its origin to Roman jurisprudence, was well known to the civil law under the more comprehensive title to compensation, which, in the words of Story, J., may be defined to be the reciprocal acquittal of debts between two person who are indebted, the one to the other; or, as it is perhaps better stated by Pothier, compensation is the extinction of debts, of which two persons are reciprocally debtors to one another, by the credits of which they are reciprocally creditors to one another. The civil law itself expressed it in a still more concise form—*compensatio est debiti et crediti inter se contributio*. The civil law treated compensation as founded upon a natural *equity*, and upon the mutual interest of each party to have the benefit of the set-off, rather than to pay what he owed, and then to have an action for what was due to himself—(Story's Eq. Juris, ss. 1438–39). The doctrine of compensation in the civil law, of course, has never been fully adopted either in England or in this country, probably for reasons based upon the inconvenience and delay which would arise in the trial of suits. But in the case before us there can be no such inconvenience or delay; the decree which declares the plaintiff pre-emptor entitled to obtain possession of the property in suit on payment of the purchase-money declares him, in the same breath,

> entitled to recovery costs from those against whom the decree has to be enforced.[18]

The reference to principles of justice, equity and good conscience coalesced with the writings of eminent jurists, such as Story, Coke, Bentham, Pothier, Savigny was typical to the adjudication style of Syed Mahmood. In the pursuit of dispensing justice, he expediently accepted that judicial legislation was at times, inevitable. He extensively quoted Justice Story, a judge of the United States Supreme Court, on equity, and referred to Story's equity jurisprudence on pleas, contracts and conflict of laws in his several judgments. His famous description of the law of limitation as a 'statute of repose' was borrowed from Justice Story's decision in *Bell v. Morrison*.[19]

In *Mangulal and others v. Kandhai Lal and another*[20] he quoted widely from Story's *Conflict of Laws* and observed, 'I adopt every word of the rules of substantial justice here laid down as distinguished from merely technical rules of procedure.'[21]

In *Lalli v. Ram Prasad*,[22] he once again turned to equity jurisprudence to rescue a party in an 'unconscionable bargain'[23] while driving home the point that operation of law should not be antithetical to the cause of advancement of justice. Quoting Justice Story, he wrote:

> [L]aw as science would be unworthy of the name if it did not to some extent provide the means of preventing the mischief of improvidence, rashness, blind confidence and credulity on one side and skill, avarice, cunning and gross violation of principles of

> morals and conscience on the other. . . . The whole system of equity jurisprudence proceeds upon the ground, that a party having a legal right, shall not be permitted to avail himself of if, for the purposes of injustice, or fraud, or oppression, or harsh and vindictive injury.[24]

He further wrote:

> I wish to add that I have considered it my duty to deliver such an elaborate judgment in this case, because I am aware that a general notion prevails in the mufaasal that ever since the repeal of the usury laws, the Courts of Justice are bound to enforce contracts as to interest, regardless of the circumstances of the case, the relative conditions of the parties, and irrespective of the unconscionableness of the bargain. Courts of Justice in India exercise the mixed jurisdiction of the Courts of Law and Equity, and in the exercise of that jurisdiction, whilst bound to respect the integrity of private contracts, they must not forget that cases which furnish adequate grounds for equitable interference must be so dealt with, not because such a course involves any the least contravention of the law, but because by reason of undue advantage having been taken of the weak and the ignorant, the contract itself is tainted with fraud in the broad sense in which that term is understood in the Courts of Equity in England and in America—a remark which seems to me fully justified by the rule of justice, equity, and good conscience, which we are bound to administer in such cases.[25]

Not only was Justice Mahmood particular about the soundness of legal reasoning in his own judgments, he also took exception to any judgment that lacked reasoning while coming up before him in appeal. Once, he took a serious note of lacklustre judicial reasoning in a judgment by a small causes judge. Admonishing the judge, he stated that the judgment was given 'in a very casual manner and it was no judgment at all, being made without appreciating the facts as well as the law.'[26]

Impressed by Mahmood's understanding of law as brought out by Indian Law Reports, Justice T. Muthuswamy Iyer, the first Indian judge of the High Court of Madras, travelled all the way to Allahabad to meet him in person.[27]

Literature and poetry were amongst the loves of his life that he invoked in his judgments, some of which are legal classics. He mastered the art of use of poetry in Arabic, Urdu, Persian and classical English literature to drive home his point. For instance, in his famous dissenting opinion in *Queen Empress v. Pohpi*[28] in 1891, he quoted a couplet from the famous Roman tragedy *Medea* (I,199) by playwright Seneca:

*Quicunque aliquid statuerit parte inaudita altera-*
*aequum licet*
*statuerit, haud aequus fuerit*

'Whoever may have decided anything, the other
side remaining unheard, granted that his decision
may have been just, will not have been just himself.'
(Translation by Justice Mahmood)

To establish that the Indian poets had embraced the same ideas as Seneca, he quoted an Urdu couplet:

*Qarib hai yaro rooze maihshar*
*Chhupega khuston ka khun kyun kar*
*Jo chup rahei zubane khanjar*
*Lahu pukarega aasteen ka*

'Oh friend! the day of judgment is near, how then will it be possible to conceal by silence the blood of those killed. Even if the tongue of the dagger will keep silence the blood on the sleeve will speak out.'

(Translation by Justice Mahmood)

Paying homage to Mahmood as a 'bright jewel', former judge of the Supreme Court of India Justice Krishna Iyer[29] remarked:

> *Justice Mahmood was great because he was just, in that imperial age when law and justice were not much in talking terms.* He was great because he was modern and dared to dissent creatively, addressing himself to tomorrow in which the nation had stakes, ignoring the dead yesterday dominated by alien spirits. He was great because he was a humanist during days when scholarship and tradition blended to inhibit learned adventures in founding fresh faiths based on the good in the old and hopes in the new. He is commemorated because he foresaw legality in the long run and forsook legalism in the short run and dedicated himself to the true rule of law for free India at a time when mental moral independence,

> even to a country as activist judicial artist was quantitatively longer than double that time as dull chopper of legal wood and so it is that Indian memory pays homage to this brief, bright jewel.[30] [emphasis added]

## Controversy with Chief Justice Edge and Resignation

After Justice Mahmood got his full appointment as a puisne judge of the Allahabad High Court in the year 1887, he got associated with Sir John Edge who was the then chief justice of the court. During these years emerged the controversy of Justice Mahmood's differences with Sir John Edge, which unfortunately culminated in the former's resignation in the year 1893.

The controversy was a subject matter of much speculation and discussion during those days. The breakdown of the relationship between Justice Mahmood and Sir John Edge is attributed to following reasons and allegations levelled against the former by the latter:

1. The participation of puisne judges (Syed Mahmood) in the administration of Court, which the Chief Justice (Sir John Edge) considered to be his exclusive domain;[31]
2. Removal of Muharram holiday from the court calendar;
3. 'Prolixity of explanation' and 'dilatoriness in delivery of reserved judgements';

4. Intemperate behaviour, sedentary habits, excessive smoking, intoxication leading to problems in court proceedings and adjudication;
5. Obstructing the administration of the high court and that his actions constituted contemptuous treatment of the court rules;
6. Inattentiveness during recording of evidence by the court, which led to the repetition of evidence and delay in trails. This, according to Sir John, irked the brother judges too.

Commenting on Mahmood's behaviour, Sir John wrote: 'Mr Justice Mahmood . . . what I can only describe as his persistent neglect of duty in and unfitness for, his office . . . He could not read the judgment being in the condition of intoxication.'[32]

On the administrative side, questions raised on the functioning of the court by Justice Mahmood were taken by Sir John as an act of defiance. On the judicial side, Mahmood's opinions dissenting from Sir John's in the cases of *Muhammad Allahadad Khan v. Ismail Khan*[33] and *Wali Ahmad Khan v. Ajudhia Kandu*[34] led to tension between the two.

Insinuating that dissentient judgments delivered by Justice Mahmood held no merit or judicial honesty, Sir John alleged that Mahmood's judgment in *Seth Chittor Mal v. Shib Lal*[35] made him regret that a judge of 'his (Syed Mahmood) reputation as a lawyer found it possible to deliver that judgment'.

Syed Mahmood summarised his perceived differences with the Chief Justice under two broad headings: differences over the running of the court, and differences over specific legal judgments. With respect to the functioning of the court, he sensed that the chief justice considered himself superior to the other puisne judges and would arbitrarily arrogate powers to make decisions regarding the rules. He described Sir John's attitude as akin to the feeling 'I am the monarch of all I survey' and commented that the chief justice was not entitled to treat his fellow judges with such an attitude.

Mahmood, conversely, insisted on his independence and equality as a judge among equals, while still recognising certain responsibilities as adhering to the office of the chief justice. He wrote:

> Now whatever views Sir John Edge may entertain with regard to this matter, [sic] in the exercise of my discretion as a Judge in revision, am surely entitled to have my separate mind and a separate conscience, and I am not bound to surrender either of them to the good wishes of the Chief Justice, who may entertain other views in regard to the exercise of such discretionary power. He has no more authority to interfere with my discretionary power in this respect than I have to interfere with his; and it can only be due to an exaggerated sense of self-importance that any Judge, whether Chief Justice or a Puisne Judge, would even attempt to interfere with his colleague's method of work.[36]

Mahmood felt Sir John had transgressed his authority in depriving him of his jurisdiction in criminal cases, first appeals and original trials. In his defence, he wrote two letters to the Chief Secretary of the NWP J.D. La Touche; in the second letter, he prayed acceptance of his resignation from office.

On the removal of holidays assigned for Muharram from the court calendar without consulting him (the only Muslim judge in the court then),[37] Mahmood alleged that Sir John considered himself racially superior and misunderstood the office of the chief justice as being autocratic in nature. He further alleged that Sir John's tendency to control things at the court made him consider any objection to his decision-making/procedural rules a threat to his authority. He also condemned the remarks made by Sir John when the former protested non-consultation on the removal of holidays assigned for Muharram. Reportedly, Sir John had remarked, '. . . to which like others, Mr Justice Mahmood ought to have been the last person to have referred.'[38]

Offended by this abrupt behaviour, Justice Mahmood reprimanded the registrar of the court who did not comply with his order. Mahmood, in disgust, said, 'Being the servant of the Judges he (registrar) was bound to even count the hair on the head of any person.'[39]

A popular Urdu daily newspaper of the time, *Najm-ul-Akhbár*, reported:

> Mr Justice Mahmood might have no objection to work during Muharram, but he was bound

> to look to the convenience of Muhammadan suitors and vakils. The interference of the Chief Justice with the Muharram holidays is regrettable and reprehensible. On the other hand, Mr Justice Mahmood is entitled to all praise for his independence, though the Congressionists will be much vexed to find that such bold and independent men still exist.[40]

On the criticism of the prolixity of explanation in his judgments, Mahmood countered that just as the length of a judgment does not embody its worth, similarly, inadequately worded judgment betrays the cause of justice. Reasoning that explaining judgments sufficiently serves the purpose of making it understandable not only to legal professionals but also to the litigants, he underscored the value of making the law (through judgments) accessible to the common man. He argued:

> I do not regard the length of a judgment as necessarily representing its value, nor do I hold that brief or inadequately expressed judgments are always the best; for I think as I have before said, a Judge in delivering judgments, especially in India, should remember that he should make his judgments full enough to be intelligible to parties and not only to trained professional lawyers.[41]

Refuting the charges of reserving judgements as a matter of habit to hinder the administration of justice, Syed Mahmood pointed out that full bench cases required elaborate arguments supported with reasons. He also clarified that because, in many cases, there was a lack of authoritative texts on substantial questions related to Indian laws, it necessitated the perusal and translation of original texts available in oriental languages. Further, he himself had to undertake this tedious task not only for himself but for his brother judges too. This task required much time and research, and therefore, the necessity for reserving judgments.[42] Justice Mahmood further argued that Sir John was not aware of the facts of native life and hence required assistance in matters pertaining to the interpretation of Indian law. He remarked:

> . . . If he (John Edge) had only allowed himself enough time to understand the Indian laws and the facts of Indian life, before assuming the position of '*veni, vidi, vici*'[43] he might have made even a better Chief Justice than he is now.[44]

Sir John Edge was caustic in his reproval of Mahmood's intemperate habits—which he perceived to have sometimes led to Mahmood's incapability in discharging judicial functions inside the courtroom—and minced no words while writing to the chief secretary of the provincial government about it, as evident in his following remark:

> The cause why Mr Justice Mahmood was sometimes incapable of attending to the evidence or arguments

> as a case proceeded, necessitating a repetition of such evidence or arguments, was that on such occasions, Mr Mahmood came to the court suffering obviously, from the results of intemperance over night. On one notorious occasion on the Judge's taking their seats in Full Bench at the sitting of the Court to deliver their judgments Mr. Justice Mahmood was, owing to his being then still in a condition of intoxication, unable to complete the reading of his prepared judgments and his judgment had to be taken as read. His condition on that occasion must have been obvious to everyone in Court.[45]

On his part, Mahmood denied in entirety the allegations of indulgence in intemperate behaviour, sedentary habits, intoxication and other immoralities. In his defence, he wrote that his personal taste was confined to books and authorship and had no inclination for any 'sports' whatsoever.

Claiming to have devoted more time to official work than any other judges who were in office then, he corroborated it through a tabular representation of the official record of judges, illustrating the exact days and hours of work performed by the judges of the high court.[46] He asserted, 'I can confidently say that I devote more time to my official work than Sir John Edge or Mr Justice Tyrell, those two gentlemen being the only remaining judges of the Court who held the office during the period to which this discussion relates.'[47]

*TABLE 3.1. Attendance record of judges from 1887 to 1892 presented by Mahmood*

| *The Hon'ble Sir John Edge* | | | *The Hon'ble Mr Justice Tyrrell* | | *The Hon'ble Justice Mahmood* | |
|---|---|---|---|---|---|---|
| Year | Dates | No of Days | Dates | No of Days | Dates | No of Days |
| 1887 | 19 April to 11 August | 115 | 19 April to 11 August | 115 | 19 April to 11 August | 115 |
| | 21 October to 31 December | 72 | 12 September to 19 October | 38 | 17 August to 12 September | 27 |
| | | | 21 October to 31 December | 72 | 21 October to 31 December | 72 |
| | Total | 187 | Total | 225 | Total | 214 |
| 1888 | 1 January to 18 August | 231 | 1 January to 18 August | 231 | 1 January to 25 February | 56 |
| | 2 November to 31 December | 60 | 15 October to 31 December | 78 | 16 March to 18 August | 156 |
| | | | | | 6 November to 31 December | 56 |
| | Total | 291 | Total | 309 | Total | 268 |
| 1889 | 15 January to 18 August | 216 | 1 January to 18 August | 230 | 1 January to 22 January | 22 |
| | 1 November to 31 December | 16 | 26 September to 31 December | 97 | 27 February to 18 August | 173 |
| | | | | | 1 November to 31 December | 61 |
| | Total | 232 | Total | 327 | Total | 256 |

| | | | | | | |
|---|---|---|---|---|---|---|
| 1890 | 1 January to 5 August<br>25 October to<br>31 December | 217<br>68 | 1 January to 31 March<br>6 November to 31 December | 90<br>56 | 1 January to 9 August<br>29 September to 31 December | 221<br>94 |
| | Total | 285 | Total | 146 | Total | 315 |
| 1891 | 1 January to 5 August<br>29 October to<br>31 December | 222<br>64 | 1 January to 10 August<br>5 October to 31 December | 222<br>88 | 1 January to 13 January<br>14 January to 8 August<br>29 October to 31 December | 13<br>176<br>64 |
| | Total | 286 | Total | 310 | Total | 253 |
| 1892 | 1 January to<br>31 December | 366 | 1 January to 19 August<br>29 October to 31 December | 232<br>64 | 1 January to 27 July<br>and 3 November | 210 |
| | Total | 366 | Total | 296 | Total | 210 |
| | Grand Total | 1692 | Grand Total | 1,613 | Grand Total | 1,516 |

*Source: Syed Mahmood's letter dated 8 September 1893 addressed to Hon'ble J.D. La Touche, Chief Secretary to the Government of NWP and Oudh*

Moreover, he argued that the harsh climate of Allahabad adversely impacted the efficiency of his work during the four months of hot weather and three to four months of rainy season. He wrote:

> In such case the fatigue to say nothing as to the irksomeness of the work, is very exhausting especially during the four months of the hot weather and during the three or four months of the rainy season which has been somewhere very aptly described by Lord Macaulay as the climate of a Turkish bath. With equal felicity of expression Sir Douglas Straight, after having sat with me in the room on the east side of the High Court building where I usually sat and where the hot West wind could not play upon the tatties to reduce the temperature of the room described the apartment as the 'Grill-room' of the Court. I confess that on occasions when I have been obliged to keep awake during the previous night to write out or complete my judgment especially in Full Bench cases, I have naturally felt very tired and sleepy the next morning, and such may possibly have been the case on the occasion in the Full Bench to which Sir John Edge refers. This state of things arises out of the fact of no previous notice being given to the Judges as to this class of work which they have to perform during the following week and especially works as a hardship personally upon me whose system of work, I frankly confess, requires elaboration of arguments and reasons especially in Full Bench cases.[48]

Syed Mahmood also complained of the inconvenience caused by the absence of any system for sufficient prior notice to the day when reserved judgments were to be delivered, as he could not sleep on nights immediately preceding the morning fixed for the delivery of judgments. On the accusation of inability to read the entire judgment in the open court on account of intoxication, he clarified that he had done so in order to save the court's time and for the convenience of the litigants, adhering to the well-established practice of the Allahabad High Court of reading only those passages which formulate the conclusions of the judge on the issues, i.e. decree or order (operative part).

Dismissing the charges of indulging in altercation and impolite behaviour as being falsely hurled at him, Mahmood retorted with the adage, 'Give a dog a bad name and he is sure to be killed.'[49] He lamented:

> I confess that the manner of treatment which I can consider neither frank nor sincere has given me more feeling of regret than I can describe, for having on many occasions accepted Sir John Edge's hospitality under the misapprehension of regarding him a personal friend.[50]

Justice Mahmood had initially planned to take legal recourse for the alleged treatment meted out to him by Sir John. This included the following steps:

1. Institute a civil suit for the recovery of damages for slander and libel,
2. Initiate criminal prosecution for defamation under Section 499 of the IPC, 1860,

3. Request for an enquiry under the Public Servants (Inquiries) Act, 1850 (XXXVII of 1850).[51]

He did not pursue this course owing to his imperfect health,[52] and the saga ended with his resignation letter addressed to the chief secretary dated 8 September 1893, which was duly accepted. After the acceptance of his resignation, the British government sanctioned him a special pension of £600 or ₹ 9,000 per annum.[53]

## Analysing the controversy

Where does the plethora of allegations and counter-allegations take us? An objective analysis of the controversy—based on a close scrutiny of the averments made against each other read with the prevailing socio-political canvas of the time—lead us into a few generalisations.

Writ large on their elaborate averments and rejoinders is that the two sides were unwilling to discuss, and in fact, they were only too keen to debate rather than communicate.

The friction between the two stemmed from the chief justice being taken aback, possibly aghast, to find his 'native' colleague's resistance to fall in line when Sir John Edge expected toeing of the line to be the natural order of things. This expectation, equally obviously, was against the grain of Mahmood, imbued as he was with the spirit of independent inquiry and free expression. But while the rudiments of the conflict originally lay in Mahmood's dissenting opinions, it thereafter conflagrated to other matters related to administrative and procedural functioning of the court.

Mahmood, it would appear, faltered in allowing his impulsive behaviour to overwhelm his ability to handle the situation with prudence in the highly hierarchical institutional frameworks of the colonial era. His weighing of criminal, civil and administrative actions against the chief justice—on which he did not follow through ultimately—precipitated the tensions. His angry missives against the chief justice were not kindly received by the higher echelons of the British administration within and outside the judicial realm. When the puisne judge was a native, the tendency to err on the side of the higher authority was almost instinctive. Moreover, the allegations against him related to his intemperate habits could not be entirely disregarded. As described in Chapter 5, Mahmood's alcohol addiction and ensuing behaviour worsened considerably towards the latter part of his life—to the extent of impairing his ability to work and estranging his relations with colleagues and family.

Nevertheless, the circumstances that forced his resignation, in which he did not let go of his and his country's honour, are indeed very lamentable. His shortcomings do not derogate from the fact his judicial integrity remained unblemished in moments of conflict—an attribute aptly conveyed in the words of former Chief Justice of India M. Hidayatullah:

> He was not one of those in whose case modesty is none else than inverted pride. It must have been

> a trying experience to be the first and lone Indian among Englishmen. He did not flinch from his duty, because to mince his words would have been fatal. Where he did not agree he boldly dissented.[54]

As a truly independent judge, Justice Mahmood simply could not accept judgeship being dependant on the 'frowns and smiles' of the chief justice who was transplanted in the Indian setup. In Para 62 of his resignation letter, he wrote, 'my furlough will expire on the 25th November next by which time I trust I shall have a reply from the Government to my application for being allowed to retire so as to enable me to form my plans for the future.'[55]

A prominent newspaper, *Hindustan* (Lucknow), of 12 October 1892 reported:

> It is very sorry that Mr Justice Mahmood has been obliged to take furlough for a year on account of ill-health. Some newspapers state that he will retire from service at the expiration of his furlough, some attribute his intended retirement to his quarrel with the Chief Justice. But such statements are without any foundation. The misunderstanding between him and the Chief Justice is not of such a serious nature as to necessitate his premature retirement.[56]

The innumerable occasions on which he dissented from his brother judges of the Allahabad High Court arose because of his uncompromising intellect that could sometimes manifest itself in ways even more strange. For instance, in Lucknow, as age-old practice, a *naubat* (drum) was sounded early morning at the China Bazaar Gate. The English deputy commissioner felt annoyed by the sound and prohibited the same. On learning about the incident, Mahmood asked the drummer to continue doing so. Afraid of sanction, he resisted, only for Mahmood to himself start on beating the drum. It is a matter of curious speculation as to what relevance the beating of the drum had for the people of Lucknow—whether it signalled a public announcement of matters relating to public interest or an alarm—which provoked Mahmood to protest against the orders of the deputy commissioner.[57]

Syed Mahmood's resignation was a disgraceful episode for his father too, who defended his son through an open letter that was carried by an Urdu newspaper. While mentioning that he never wanted his son to be a judge in the first place, he saw it as an episode of 'Englishmen robbing Indian civil servants of their self-respect'. He wrote:

> In my opinion the time is not yet, and will perhaps never be, that our European friends who are the conquerors of this country and who have the ascendancy and superiority natural to conqueror, and Indian, who are the vanquished and are held in the contempt natural for the vanquished, can both sit together on the same bench and function with equal honour and pride, suitable to the rank that they both hold. If the Indian maintains his self-respect which he should, were he to answer the demands of honesty and good breeding, then the life of both parties continues to be hard and bitter . . . it is not at all a secret now that there is a difference of black and

> white between how English treat their own community and how they treat others. . . . [Syed Mahmood] gets no pleasure in positions of power. Rather, he looks down upon power and considers it knavish to feel pride in a job with the Government.[58]

The personal indignation he felt even led him to mull over ending his deep-rooted project of friendship with the British. Not only did he comfort himself with the fact that his son had mustered the courage to stand up to the British but he also saw it as a moment when, finally, his son would come to Aligarh to take up the work that he originally wished him to do.

## Litigant-Friendly Judge

Justice Mahmood was known to be compassionate towards the litigants. He was especially considerate towards litigants who could not make it to the hearing on time on account of geographical distances. From the incidents reported in the dailies, it is known that he treated litigants with utmost respect, especially women and relatives of the former monarchs.

*Halat-e-Hind* Allahabad reported an account of the alleged ill-treatment of Amir Jahan Begam by Mr Cobb, city magistrate of Lucknow (3 February 1891), terming it tyrannical. It stated:

> European Magistrates are ready to disgrace even one's mother and sisters. Her Gracious Majesty [sic] has sent them to this country to protect the

> lives and property of the people and not to ill-treat them. Often European ladies have occasion to appear before native Magistrates or Judges, they are always treated with respect. *Look at the respectful way in which Mr. Justice Mahmood behaves towards the European lady whose case is pending before him at present.* On the other hand, European officers do not hesitate to ill-treat most respectable ladies of ex-royal families.[59] [emphasis added]

The vernacular newspaper *Azad* (Lucknow) reported about the courtesy extended by Justice Syed Mahmood, then the district judge of Raebareli, to Raja Ajit Singh[60] who once appeared before him to give evidence in a case.[61]

Being an able speaker with a tendency to ratiocinate and persuade, Mahmood could easily make *justitia*[62] and litigants smile in satisfaction while he read his judgments in open court.

An amusing anecdote during Syed Mahmood's tenure as a judge is mentioned through an experience of his father, Sir Syed. During those days, Indians were not allowed to travel in first-class compartments of Indian Railways, all of which were reserved for Englishmen. Once, Sir Syed entered such a compartment and found an Englishman sitting there. 'Why have you come here?' the Englishman angrily asked; Sir Syed, instead of introducing himself, asked him, 'Why are you here, Sir?' On hearing his reply 'I am a judge', Sir Syed retorted, '*Maein judge ka baap hoon*' (literally, I am a judge's father, but figuratively meaning, I am superior to you).[63]

## Involvement in Legislative Drafting

Mahmood's versatility in law, besides as a lawyer, teacher and judge, also extended to his involvement in legislative drafting.

He assisted Sir Syed Ahmad Khan when the latter was a member of the viceroy's Legislative Council, in drafting the Muslim Family Waqf Bill, 1879. In this bill, Sir Syed mooted the introduction of the concept of *Waqf-alal-aulad*[64] to prevent the disintegration of property.[65] In the aftermath of the revolt of 1857, the colonial government, in exercise of its retribution, set upon the task of expropriating immovable properties of Muslims, especially lands. The affluent Muslims owning sizeable lands, in order to escape the state policy of retribution, resorted to disposing them at rates much below their value. The fragmentation of property was considered one of the major contributing factors in the decline of the Muslim landed elite with what he saw as the cast-iron enforcement of the Muslim law of succession under the British.[66] Mahmood's firm grounding in Muslim law helped Sir Syed propose a law that would confer legal recognition on the Islamic concept of *Waqf*—a system wherein Muslims are endowed with an option to convert their property into a trust by vesting its ownership in God. This mechanism forecloses the right of an inheritor to sell or transfer it, thereby preventing fragmentation.

In 1882, Mahmood impressed the venerated English jurist, Sir Fredrick Pollock, with his memorandum prepared for revising the draft of a proposed Civil Wrongs Bill for the Government of India.

Complimenting his efforts, Sir Pollock remarked that the memorandum was carefully prepared and incorporated some 'good suggestions'.[67]

As a high court judge, Justice Mahmood made key suggestions in the India High Courts Bill, 1888—introduced to supplement the Indian High Courts Act of 1861.

On jurisdiction, he argued for empowerment of the Crown to enable it to extend territorial jurisdiction of the high courts in India and increase the jurisdiction of single benches in civil disputes.[68] He further expressed concern that the rules of the high court, as applicable then, attached greater importance to property over a person's life and liberty. He criticised the practice of dismissal of appeals without any hearing by the courts in case of failure of the appellant to deposit the cost of the English translation of the order/judgment. In his view, the fee charged was exorbitant and impeded justice by taking a toll on the appellant. He believed that language bar should not be a barrier to the dispensation of justice. For the larger benefit and convenience of native Indian lawyers, he proposed that the law should empower the governor general in council to declare official languages of high courts from time to time, and thus, suggested that the draft bill should contain a provision to this effect. To facilitate the process of administration of justice, he also recommended employment of interpreters for the courts.[69]

He is also credited to have written a minute on the Guardians and Wards Bill, 1890, in which he argued against the interference of legislative laws in the domain of personal laws, such as those regulating relations between a guardian and their ward.[70]

It was on Mahmood's insistence that the Village Courts Bill, 1892, for NWP and Oudh was passed, which provided for the establishment of arbitral tribunals of local notables in villages for the settlement of minor disputes. A noted Urdu daily of the time, *Alam-i-Taswir* (Cawnpore, 16 August 1892), advertising the Village Courts Bill for NWP and Oudh, observed that poor villagers would greatly benefit by the tribunals, and that they should be grateful to Justice Mahmood who earnestly pressed the necessity for the establishment of such tribunals on the government.[71]

# 4

# Landmark Judgments

While there are many dimensions of Mahmood's life, he is most well known as a judge of the Allahabad High Court from 1887 to 1893. As noted earlier, prior to that—from 1882 to 1887—he served as a temporary judge intermittently on four separate occasions. As a high court judge, his 383 judgments are reported in the Indian Law Reports.[1] However, this is not the total number of judgments delivered by him, but only those which were considered as noteworthy expositions on substantial questions of law and formed valuable sources for further judicial precedents. The total number of his judgments are known to be more than 3,000.[2]

When he finally resigned from his office as a judge under acrimonious circumstances in 1893, he had built an accomplished record of judgments, which are admired for their jurisprudential scholarship. The sphere of his judgments covered not only Muslim law but also the wide remit of procedure law, limitation, transfer of property, torts, land laws, Hindu law, evidence, equity, adoption, professional ethics, succession laws, etc.

This chapter captures his grand contribution to law through a glimpse of his selected judgments. However, selecting his 'select judgments'—which can be termed as 'landmark'—was a challenging task. The said challenge lay in determining the criteria for selecting these judgments—impact on society, jurisprudential scholarship, protecting civil liberty, advancement of justice, precedential value or reliance by future courts, laying down the law on issues of paramount importance, interpretative approach, contemporary relevance, etc. In all, this chapter analyses 22 of his judgments—out of which 11 are dissenting—that are seminal for one or more reasons illustrated above.

On the significance of the judgments delivered by Justice Mahmood as a high court judge, former Chief Justice K. Subba Rao, while unveiling the portrait of Justice Mahmood at the centenary celebration programme of the Allahabad High Court on 27 November 1966 said the following words:

> I deem it an honour to unveil the portrait of one of the greatest Judges that our country has produced, Mr Justice Mahmood . . . . His judgments are masterly exposition[s] on the different subjects dealt with by him. They reflect research, scholarship, hard work and thoroughness in detail. Some of his judgments hold the field even now though a century has passed since they were delivered . . .
>
> Only a few are respected both by the contemporaries and by posterity. He was one of those few; and the public esteem which he enjoyed during his lifetime has not abated but indeed has cast a halo around him. He was one of the typical Judges of our country who brought about synthesis between ancient Hindu and Muhammadan laws [sic] and the Common law imported directly or through statutes from England. His dissenting judgments expounding

> principles of natural justice—a man who asserts a right has a right to be heard evolving the concept of property—it includes the equity of redemption and laying down the doctrine—procedural laws are subservient to substantive laws reflect his equitable and balanced approach to the legal problems. His judgments propounding that on the death of a Muhammadan intestate, his estate devolved on his heir, notwithstanding the existence of debts, that an offspring of adultery could not be made legitimate by acknowledgment of the putative father, and that the law of pre-emption was not a personal right, but was a right of substitution, are masterpieces of erudition and products of an analytical mind. His exposition of the doctrine of salvage, and the extension of it both to the perils of sea and perils of land discloses an original mind . . . .
>
> He was a man of vision and philosophy of his own. Rule of law to him was not an instrument of tyranny, but was the soothing touch to the inflicted and oppressed. Whether in the matter of construction of a provision of a statute or in elucidating a doctrine of Muhammadan law [sic], he did not adopt a wooden attitude but evolved principles to guide the future. To him the rule of law was a way of life.[3]

The book *Anglo-Indian Codes* by Sir Whitley Stokes—a law member of the Council of the Governor-General of India during the years 1877 to 1882—mentions, 'No judgments in the whole series of Indian Law Reports are more weighty and illuminating than those of Justice Syed Mahmood.'[4]

## A Humane Judge

In essence, Mahmood's judgments stand out for putting human beings and humanity at the centre of his legal universe. This quality of his is resonated in the words of Justice V.R. Krishna Iyer, former judge of the Supreme Court of India:

> The rule of law finds the finest hour when it runs close to the rule of life. Erudition in a judge, without this social perspective, is like [a] large library with all doors closed to the readers. Mahmood was so learned that his discussions of legal issues winged into the vast without dwelling narrowly in the small nest of the facts of the case.[5]

In the case of *Queen Empress v. Pohpi*,[6] Justice Mahmood observed that a 'fair trial' is integral to a just legal system. Though it has now become fashionable to locate the fair trial values in the constitution alone, he had the prescience during the colonial era to recognise 'fair trial' as an essential part of the criminal justice system.[7]

In this case, an appeal was made to Justice Mahmood's court against the judgment of a subordinate court sentencing five accused persons to ten years of rigorous imprisonment. The accused were neither represented by a lawyer nor were they released from jail to appear before the court in person. Ordinarily, such appeals were dismissed without 'hearing' the accused.

This case became famous for Justice Mahmood's dissent regarding the term 'hearing' in Section 423 of the Code of Criminal Procedure, 1882. According to this provision:

Section 423: Powers of Appellate Court in disposing of appeal

(1) *The Appellate Court shall then send for the record of the case, if such record is not already in Court. After perusing such record, and 'hearing' the appellant or his pleader, 'if he appears', and the Public Prosecutor, if he appears, and, in case of an appeal under section 417, the accused, if he appears, the Court may, if it considers that there is no sufficient ground for interfering, dismiss the appeal*, or may—

(a) in an appeal from an order of acquittal, reverse such order and direct that further inquiry be made, or that the accused be retried or committed for trial, as the case may be, or find him guilty and pass sentence on him according to law;

(b) in an appeal from a conviction, (1) reverse the finding and sentence, and acquit or discharge the accused, or order him to be retried by a Court of competent jurisdiction subordinate to such Appellate Court or committed for trial, or (2) alter the finding, maintaining the sentence, or, with or without altering the finding, reduce the sentence, or, (3) with or without such reduction and with or without altering the finding, alter the nature of the sentence but, subject to the provisions of section 106, sub-section (3), not so as to enhance the same;

(c) in an appeal from any other order, alter or reverse such order;

> (d) make any amendment or any consequential or incidental order that may be just or proper. [emphasis added]

The majority opinion given by Chief Justice Edge was that in cases where the accused is neither present in person nor represented by a lawyer, then all that can be done by the court is to peruse the record of the accused for deciding the case.

Justice Mahmood held the existing law to be in violation of the principles of natural justice. He recognised the two basic doctrines of human jurisprudence—*audi alteram partem* (hear the other side) and *ubi jus ibi remedium* (where there is a right, there is a remedy)—and held that the court had the power to order the release of the accused from jail and brought to the court for defending himself in person.

In dealing with the question of when a notice (to the accused) is deemed served, he observed:

> I have got to deal with the word '*notice*' and the object of its being used with the specification of time and place at which such appeal will be heard. Did the legislature [sic] intend by using these words that the person to whom such notice was to be given was to be tied by the leg by actual iron chains so as to disable him from avoiding the result, namely, the dismissal of his appeal and yet give him notice? I cannot hold any such tiling, I find it impossible to do so, for then S. 422 (notice of appeal) would never have existed, for

> the whole section in most cases would have been a surplusage. The last part of that section also leads to the same conclusion, because there the case contemplated is an appeal presented not by the prisoner but by the Crown, under the special powers given to it by section 417 [appeal on behalf of government in case of acquittal], against a verdict of acquittal.[8]

Appearing to have draped himself in the robes of an advocate pleading for justice, Justice Mahmood, in his spirited dissent, further had this to say:

> Having so far dealt with these aspects of the case, as they have appeared to me both in point of law and upon points which I think have even higher basis than that doubtful phrase, I think it is necessary for me to say that, if it is true that the law of British India makes it possible for me sitting here as a Judge, in the first place, *by dint of my writ to order a person to be imprisoned and tied by the chain, then in the next place to require the mockery of asking him to attend when I, by dint of the exercise of my own power, have made it impossible for him to attend and then have the solemn mockery of having his name called out*, if this is the law of British India, I hope the sooner it is abrogated the better.
>
> *I am of the opinion that we cannot proceed to hear this case, unless the prisoners are before us, or can be heard* within the meaning of section 423 of the Criminal Procedure Code.[9] [emphasis added]

Chief Justice Edge stopped assigning Mahmood criminal cases on the latter's refusal to hear criminal appeals unless the appellant appeared in court or had legal representation.

Interestingly, the writer of the foreword of this book, Justice Sudhanshu Dhulia, while deciding a rape appeal in *Kalwa v. State of Uttarakhand*[10] before the Uttarakhand High Court in 2018, where the accused had no meaningful defence at the trial stage, has very tellingly referred to a full bench judgment of the Allahabad High Court in 1891, *Queen Empress v. Pohpi*. Invoking Justice Mahmood's 'real hearing' as an essential ingredient of a fair trial seemed to have enabled Justice Dhulia not only to allow the appeal and set aside the conviction but also to indulge in knowledge generation by taking us back to the roots of the concept of a fair criminal trial itself.

Former Chief Justice of the Supreme Court, Justice Manepalli Narayana Rao Venkatachaliah, also commended Mahmood's judgment. He wrote in 2012:

> *One sterling example in India is Justice Mahmood who, in 1891, enunciated the essentials of natural justice and the consequences of its non-observance.* In a dissenting opinion in a full bench case, he held that a criminal appeal under section 423 [sic] of the Code of Criminal Procedure [sic] against conviction could not be decided without hearing the imprisoned accused in person if he was unrepresented by a lawyer because without that requirement the appeal could not be treated as heard.[11] [emphasis added]

On another occasion, once, when a superintendent of police brought a handcuffed prisoner in his court, Justice Mahmood, who found it against the law, rebuked him saying, 'How could you bring someone in Her Majesty's Court of Justice in irons?'[12]

Justice Mahmood is famous for his courageous advocacy for human rights at a time when law and justice did not appear to be on the same page.

In the case of *Queen Empress v. Babulal,*[13] he recorded his dissent from the majority view. The case related to putting checks on torture of prisoners for extraction of confessions under the Indian Evidence Act, 1872.[14] Under the law of evidence, as a general rule, the confession made by a person in custody of a police officer is inadmissible in evidence, unless made in the immediate presence of an officer mandated by law. The presence of such officers acts as a check upon maltreatment of the prisoners.

His trailblazing dissent proposed to put a stop on the extortion of confessions by taking away from the police officers the advantage of providing such extorted confessions during the trial of accused persons.

Mahmood is also recognised for treating issues of substantive justice on a higher pedestal vis-à-vis procedural technicalities. Through his novel legal acumen and interpretation, he championed for the weaker sections of the Indian society, as in the case of *Parbati v. Bhola.*[15] The case related to the law of limitation that prescribes a time-limit for different suits within which an aggrieved person can approach the court for justice. He opined that the operation of the limitation law unreasonably discriminated against a poor litigant, as the balance of benefit of a legal remedy was more accessible to the rich than the poor. Hence, it failed substantive justice in favour of procedural technicalities.[16]

## Muslim Law Judgments

Commenting on Mahmood's remarkable intellectual might in Muslim law, Justice M. Hidayatullah said:

> No judge before Syed Mahmood or since has shown such an acquaintance with the fundamentals of Muslim Law . . . He has taken unprecedented pains to refer Sharayul Islam, Maftih, Ashbab, Fakhrul Islama, Bazdawi, Fathul Qadir, Durrul Mukhtar, Fatwa i Alamgiri, Shamsul Aimma, Zahirul Rewayat, Fatawai Hind, Suri Viqayah, Al Sirajiyah, Kifaya, Muhitus Sarkhasi, Raddul Mukhtar, Fatwa Kazi Khan, Birjindi, Muslim, Aini, Khassaf, Abu Zaid. He is known to have compared the standard works of Baillie, Grady, Hamilton, Rumsey and others and if could not find a satisfying translation, he would do that himself. Even the text books which one reads today do not contain references to these authoritative works of Sunni and Shia laws.[17]

Early on in his judicial career, when he was a district judge at Raebareli, a letter of Mahmood dated 15 June 1881 addressed to Lieutenant Colonel P.D. Henderson—then posted in India as general superintendent of Operations for the Suppression of Thuggee and Dacoity—gives an insight into his deep understanding of Muslim personal law. In Mahmood's view, the political context had largely impacted the content of Muslim law, hinting at the Republican system of governance under Prophet Muhammad (P.B.U.H.) and the succeeding caliphate. Arguably, in reference to inheritance law, he did not imply the law as being secular in nature but the idea that monarchs who followed the four caliphs retained the original law of inheritance owing to its origin in the Holy Koran.[18]

Justice Mahmood's decision in *Amir Muhammad Khan v. Jafri Begam*[19] is regarded as an innovation in Muslim law. It led to the formulation of a standard theory on an important facet of 'Muslim law relating to inheritance' that paved the way for significant judicial reform in the *Hanafi* law relating to the administration of estates.

In this case, the issue before the full bench related to the devolution of ownership of property that is encumbered by debt on the heirs of Muhammadan 'intestate'—a term designating a person who has died without leaving a will. The question was whether upon the death of a Muhammadan intestate who leaves unpaid debts with reference to the value of his estate, should ownership devolve immediately on his heirs or whether devolution be contingent upon the payment of such debts. This issue was vexing in that the views of the different high courts seemed to contradict some of the principles of Muhammadan jurisprudence.

Mahmood ruled that Muhammadan heirs are independent owners of their specific shares, and if they take their shares subject to the charge of the debts of the deceased, their liability is in proportion to the extent of their shares.

According to him, the devolution of inheritance on the heirs of the deceased was to be determined at the point of moment of death of the owner. The presence of debt, irrespective of its size, was irrelevant. Whatever be the size or character of the debt, the property of the deceased is liable to its payment, and though its size regulates the balance of the estate, it, in no way, hinders the fact of devolution. The position of law was in contrast with that of Hindu co-heirs in a joint family.

In deciding the issue, he relied upon the interpretation of Koran as accepted by noted Islamic jurists and undertook a comprehensive investigation of Muhammadan law sources through *Hedaya*, *al-Sirājīyah* and *Baizwani*.

*Hedaya* is a 12th-century work authored by the leading Muslim jurist, Burhan al-Din al-Marghinani. The original Arabic *al-Hidāyah* remains a central text of Islamic personal law for those Muslims governed by the *Hanafi* school of jurisprudence—a group that constitutes an overwhelming majority of Muslims in south Asia and large parts of central Asia. An English translation from a Persian version of the work was prepared by the orientalist Charles Hamilton for the East India Company in 1791 and was used by British courts. Mahmood, however, referred to the original work instead of the translated version.

*Kitāb al-Farā'iḍ al-Sirājīyah* or the Sirajite book of inheritance laws is regarded as the most important treatise on the laws of inheritance according to the Hanafi School of Sunni Islamic jurisprudence, which is followed by the majority of the Muslim community in India.

*Baizwani*, also known as *Tafsir al-Baydawi*, is one of the most popular classic Sunni Koranic interpretational works (*tafsir*) composed by the 13th-century Muslim scholar Al-Baydawi.

Mahmood's scrutiny of these original texts enabled him to illuminate unexplored areas of Muhammadan law on the issue of Muslim intestate.

In his judgment, he lamented that some of the highest tribunals in India repeatedly expressed views upon the subject, which directly contradicted some of the principles of Muhammadan jurisprudence as understood then. His judgment removed the cloud cast by earlier erroneous exposition upon various aspects of Muhammadan law.

His landmark decision in the case of *Gobind Dayal v. Inayatullah*[20] is considered the most authoritative exposition on an important concept under the Muhammadan law relating to property—law of pre-emption.

The judgment of the full bench was delivered by Justice Mahmood with whom all the present judges agreed. According to Justice Mahmood's definition:

> Pre-emption is a right which the owner of certain immovable property possesses, as such, for the quiet enjoyment of that immovable property, to obtain, in substitution for the buyer, proprietary possession of certain other immovable property, not his own, on such terms as those, on which such latter immovable property is sold to another person.[21]

His contribution through this judgment lay in according clarity on the issue of cross-religious application of the Muhammadan law doctrine of pre-emption. In particular, the question related to the applicability of pre-emption in situations where not all parties are Muslims.

In this case, the pre-emptor[22] and the vendor[23] of the property were Muslims and the vendee[24] a Hindu. The question was whether in such a case the right of pre-emption could be enforced against a non-Muslim, that is, the Hindu, in this case.

To answer this question, he dwelled on the nature and origin of the right of pre-emption and observed the following:

1. The Hindu and Muslim laws are so intimately connected with religion that they cannot readily be dissevered from each other.
2. The law of pre-emption is essentially a part of Muslim jurisprudence and has been introduced to India by Muslim judges who were bound to administer Muslim law. It thus became for centuries the common law of the country and was applied universally to Hindus and Muslims; however, Hindus adopted it as a custom.

Illustrating the possible situations, he clarified the following:

1. If all the parties were Muslims, Muslim law applies.
2. If all the parties are Hindu, Muslim law does not apply.
3. If the vendor and vendee are Hindu but the pre-emptor is Muslim, there is no pre-emption.

4. If the pre-emptor is Hindu and the vendor and vendee are Muslim, there is no pre-emption.
5. If the vendee is Muslim and the pre-emptor and vendor a Hindu, there is no pre-emption.
6. If the vendor is Muslim and the pre-emptor and the vendee are Hindu, there is no pre-emption. This is so because now Muslim law is a personal law and not the common law of the land, and the rights and obligations must be reciprocal.
7. If the pre-emptor and the vendee are Muslim but the vendee a Hindu, the right of pre-emption arises.

As regards the nature of the right of pre-emption and its accrual, he pointed out:

> Right of pre-emption under the Muhammadan Law is not a *right of re-purchase* either from the vendor or from the vendee, involving any new contract of sale; but it is simply a *right of substitution*, entitling the pre-emptor, by reason of a legal incident to which the sale itself was subject, to stand in the shoes of the vendee in respect of all the rights and obligations arising from the sale under which he has derived his title. It is, in effect, as if in a sale-deed the vendee's name were rubbed out and the pre-emptor's name inserted in its place.

To support his observations, he relied on the sayings of the Prophet (P.B.U.H.) on pre-emption in respect of every joint undivided property as reported in *Aini* (well-known book on Muhammadan jurisprudence) and *Muslim* (collection of Hadith or sayings of the Prophet on Muslim law):

1. *Aini*: It is not lawful for anyone to sell till he has informed his coparcener who may take or leave it as he wishes; and if he has sold without such information, the coparcener has a preferential right to the share.
2. *Muslim*: Pre-emption exists in all joint properties, whether land, or house, or grove. It is not proper for him (the owner) to sell till he has offered it to his coparcener, who may take or reject it; and if the vendor fails to do this, his coparcener has the preferential right to it until he is informed.

He also elaborated that because pre-emption is governed by Muslim law, which is derived from the Koran and Hadith, the contestations surrounding such rights must also be decided according to the principles of Muslim law and not of equity. He opined that equity cannot invent rules to govern rights that fall in the strict domain of Muslim law.

Recently in 2020, the Hon'ble Supreme Court of India has in *Raghunath (D) v. Radha Mohan (D) and Others*[25] affirmed the decision of Justice Mahmood in *Gobind Dayal v. Inayatullah*.[26]

Further, in the landmark case of *Shayara Bano v. Union of India*[27] wherein the practice of triple-talaq was declared unconstitutional by the Supreme Court in 2017, Justice Rohinton Nariman quoted Syed Mahmood's observation in Gobind Dayal's case, 'It is to be remembered that Hindu and Muhammadan laws are so intimately connected with religion that they cannot readily be dissevered from each other.'[28]

Justice Mahmood, through his erudition and scholarship, adjudicated upon issues for resolving intersectional differences amongst various sects of Muslims. Muslims in their practice of Islam adhere to various sects or schools of doctrine, differing from each other, either in matters of principle or in matters of detail as to the minor points of ritual. Majorly, there are four schools founded by the four orthodox imams, namely, Abu Hanifa, Malik, Shafai and Hanbal, all of whom flourished within the first two centuries of the Muhammadan era (8th century of the Christian era).

Mahmood adjudicated upon issues pertaining to the performance of congregational prayer at public mosques. The issues were:

1. Whether Muslims of different sects can, as a matter of right, offer prayer in a public mosque built by one of the sects of Muslims?
2. Whether pronouncing the word *amin*[29] loudly[30] during the prayers at public mosque amounts to disturbing a religious assembly—an offence punishable under Section 296[31] of the Indian Penal Code, 1860?

The first question whether a public mosque is open for worship to all Muslims irrespective of the difference in the manner of offering of namaz in different sects came to be considered before a full bench of the Allahabad High Court in *Jangu and others v. Ahmad Ullah and others.*[32] The matter involved the right of a *ghair muqallid* Muslim to utter the word *amin* aloud in a congregation of Hanafis, who utter it in silence. Mahmood held that in a public mosque, all Muhammadans are entitled to offer prayer.

With this, he referred with approval his earlier decision in *Queen-Empress v. Ramzan*[33] and ruled that the ownership of a mosque vests in God, and not in any individual. He observed:

> . . . a Mosque when public is not the property of any particular individual or even a body or corporation of any other human organisation which in the law has a personality. In the eye of the Muhammadan law a Mosque is the property of God, it must be recognised as such, and subject only to such limitations as the Muhammadan ecclesiastical law itself provides, it is public property, being the property of God for the use of his servants, and every human being is entitled to go and worship there so long as he conforms to the rules of the Muhammadan ecclesiastical ritual of worship.[34]

The second issue was on the conflict between Islamic law and criminal law. Mahmood granted precedence to Islamic law while reasoning that the matter was not a criminal one—causing disturbance in a place of worship—but was governed by the rules of *fiqh*, that is, Islamic legal interpretation.

He observed that the case does not prove that the accused uttered the word *amin* aloud with the intention of disturbing the rest of the congregation and was also justified in law to exercise their right of worship within the meaning of Section 79 of the Indian Penal Code. Section 79 reads:

> Act done by a person justified, or by mistake of fact believing himself justified, by law: Nothing is an

> offence which is done by any person who is justified by law, or who by reason of a mistake of fact and not by reason of a mistake of law in good faith, believes himself to be justified by law, in doing it.

The decision in *Ata-Ullah and another v. Azim-Ullah and another*[35] was rendered by a five-judge bench of the Allahabad High Court the very next day after the full bench judgment in *Jangu v. Ahmad Ullah*[36] was rendered.

In this case, a mosque was built by the Hanafi sect of Muhammadans and used as their place of worship since inception. Plaintiffs who described themselves as Wahabis, sought to offer prayer in the above mosque, which was objected to by defendants saying that the system of prayer of the two is different; therefore, plaintiffs cannot offer prayer in the mosque established by the Hanafi sect.

Answering a similar question as to whether Muhammadans of different sects as a matter of right can offer prayer in a public mosque built by another sect of Muhammadans, Justice Mahmood in his concurring but separate judgment again reiterated his observations in *Queen Empress v. Ramzan*:[37]

> . . . so long as a mosque is a mosque, that so long as the plaintiffs are persons who call themselves Muhammadans and [are] entitled to worship, there is absolutely no authority to say that any sect or any creed or any portion of the community can restrain others who claim to have the right which to use the language of Muhammadan law, God and

his Prophet gave them, from putting such right into exercise.[38]

Justice Mahmood is reported to have admonished the advocate appearing for appellants in the case of *Queen Empress v. Ramzan* for referring to the mosque under dispute as a 'Hanafi mosque'. To him, mosque was a house that belonged to the Almighty, and therefore, no sect could claim or earmark it as subscribing to its ideology or ethos.

In his concurring but separate decision *in Muhammad Allahadad Khan v. Muhammad Ismail Khan*,[39] Mahmood clarified the position of Muslim law relating to legitimacy of children and acknowledgement of paternity. The issue before the court was whether acknowledgement by father confers legitimacy on a Muslim child whose paternity was not proved, for the purposes of inheritance from the father's estate. The paternity of a child is in question when either the fact of the marriage itself or the exact time of its occurrence with reference to the legitimacy of the acknowledged child is not proved in the sense of the law as distinguished from being disproved.

Embarking upon a comparative analysis of the doctrine of adoption as understood under the Roman, French and Scottish legal systems and the doctrine of acknowledgement of paternity under the Muslim law, Justice Mahmood underscored the social purpose of law.

Referring to authoritative Islamic law texts on the subject, he concluded that acknowledgment of parentage by the father of a child was not similar to adoption (a concept recognised under the Roman and Hindu legal systems), and Muslim law does not recognise adoption as a mode of filiation—the fact of being the child of a particular parent(s).

Distinguishing the status of a child whose paternity is *not proved* from an illegitimate child born out of 'zina' or illicit intercourse, he pointed out:

> . . . that under the Muhammadan law of inheritance, in no case can an illegitimate child, that is, the offspring of *zina* or illicit intercourse, be entitled to inheritance from his father or through him, because he is regarded as nullius filius, i.e., a person whose *nusub* or descent from the father is wanting.[40]

Describing the exact place which *ikrar* or acknowledgement in general occupies in Muhammadan jurisprudence, Justice Syed Mahmood posed the question whether Section 112[41] of the Evidence Act, 1872 had the effect of superseding the contrary provisions of Muslim personal law. However, he left the question open.

He concluded that acknowledgement by the father had the effect of conferring the status of a son on a legitimate child for the purpose of inheritance from his (father's) estate.

Mahmood's progressive explanation of the doctrine of acknowledgement of paternity under Muslim law stands tall as an authority on the subject even today in India as well as in other South Asian jurisdictions of Pakistan and Bangladesh. Appreciating the erudition of Mahmood's judgment in this case, Justice V.R. Krishna

Iyer wrote, 'the erudite comparison with other systems of law to grasp the genius of the Muhammadan Law is an example for the present judicial generation of placing learning at the service of law.'[42]

Sohaira Siddiqui of the Georgetown University has made a scholarly analysis of Mahmood's judgment in this case. Her study finds that through this judgment, Mahmood successfully brought to fore the inherent contradictions in applying English legal rules in adjudication of Islamic Law doctrines; in as much as the English Law distinction between procedural and substantive law is oblivious to Islamic Law. This contradiction in the character of two legal traditions became a flashpoint in this case—with the prospect of English evidence law (procedural) superseding a substantive issue of Islamic Law. While Mahmood's legal acuity deserves praise for identifying this dilemma, it must be noted that by not answering the question, he did not resolve it—probably because he concluded that the issue was principally regarding interpretation of Islamic law, and the law of evidence was not applicable. In any case, the point was resolved after the full enforcement of the Evidence Act of 1872.[43]

Siddiqui is surprised at Mahmood's limited engagement with the law of evidence in this case, given that he had written a book on the subject. However, she incorrectly notes that Mahmood's book on law of evidence was published only a year before his judgment in this case in 1888.[44] The book was published in 1876 and was later reprinted in Hyderabad in 1887. Moreover, Siddiqui's speculation that 'Mahmood is tight-lipped in his critique of the British codes as it would have risked his judicial position'[45] seems to be tenuous in view of his dissents in several other cases on British codes.

Justice Mahmood's judgment in *Abdul Kadir v. Salima*[46] was an inflexion point in the interpretation of the Muslim law on marriage by the Indian courts. Most of his observations were later incorporated in the Muslim law of marriage.

In the judgment, he discussed in detail the following aspects of Muslim law on marriage:

1. Nature of a Muslim marriage,
2. Liability of the husband to pay dower,
3. Matrimonial rights of husband and wife.

He settled controversial questions on the nature of Muslim marriage by holding that a Muslim marriage is *not a sacrament but a contract*.

Employing the language used by Shama Churun Sircar in his Tagore Law Lecture[47] *The Mohammedan Law: Being a Digest of the Law Applicable Especially to Sunnis in India* in 1873, Justice Mahmood explained the nature of Muslim marriage as:

> . . . I adopt the language employed in the Tagore Law Lectures (1873) in saying that marriage among Muhammadans is not a sacrament, but purely a civil contract; and though it is solemnised generally with recitation of certain verses from the Koran[sic], yet the Muhammadan law does not positively prescribe any service peculiar to the occasion. That it is a civil contract is manifest from the various ways and circumstances in and under which marriages are contracted or presumed

> to have been contracted. And though a civil contract, it is not positively prescribed to be reduced to writing, but the validity and operation of the whole are made to depend upon the declaration or proposal of the one, and the acceptance or consent of the other, of the contracting parties, or of their natural and legal guardians before competent and sufficient witnesses; as also upon the restrictions imposed, and certain of the conditions required to be abided by according to the peculiarity of the case.[48]

Further, he also clarified that the contractual nature of a Muslim marriage did not make the dower a *price or consideration for sale*. He inferred that the comparison between 'dower' and 'price in the contract of sale' made by Arabic textbooks on Muhammadan law was simply to illustrate the incidents of other contracts by analogy. He opined:

> . . . if the authors of the Arabic text-books of Muhammadan law have compared it to price in the contract of sale, it is simply because *marriage is a civil contract under that law, and sale is the typical contract which Muhammadan jurists are accustomed to refer to in illustrating the incidents of other contracts by analogy*. Such being the nature of the dower, the rules which regulate its payment are necessarily affected by the position of a married woman under the Muhammadan law. Under that law marriage does not make her property of the husband, nor does coverture impose any disability upon her as to freedom of contract. The marriage contract is easily

dissoluble, and the freedom of divorce and the rule of polygamy place a power in the hands of the husband which the law-giver intended to restrain by rendering the rules as to payments of dower stringent upon the husband. No limit as to the amount of dower has been imposed, and it may either be prompt, that is immediately payable upon demand, or deferred, that is payable upon the dissolution of marriage, whether by death or divorce. The dower may also be partly prompt and partly deferred; but when at the time of the marriage ceremony no specification in this respect is made, the whole dower is presumed to be prompt and due on demand.[49] [emphasis added]

Justice Mahmood also illustrated the legal effects of a Muslim marriage as below:

1. It legalises the enjoyment of husband and wife with each other in the manner which in this matter is permitted by the law,
2. It subjects the wife to the power of restraint, that is, she becomes prohibited from going out and appearing in public,
3. It renders her dower, maintenance and raiment obligatory on him,
4. It establishes on both sides the prohibitions of affinity and the rights of inheritance, and the obligatoriness of justness between the wives and their rights,
5. It imposes on the wife submission to husband when summoned to the couch,
6. It confers on husband the power of correction when the wife is disobedient or rebellious, and enjoins

upon him associating familiarly with her with kindness and courtesy,

7. It renders unlawful the conjunction of two sisters (as wives) and of those who fall under the same category.

On the edifice of Baillie's *Digest of Moohummudan Law* and Hamilton's *Hedaya*, he observed that the dower under Muhammadan law cannot be regarded as the consideration for connubial intercourse. On the question as to when does the right of cohabitation accrue, Mahmood answered that the right of cohabitation comes into existence at the same time and by reason of the same incident of law as the right of dower. He observed:

> . . . *that the right of cohabitation comes into existence at the same time and by reason of the same incident of law as the right of dower*. Dower, under the Muhammadan law, is a sum of money or other property promised by the husband to be paid or delivered to the wife in consideration of the marriage, and even where no dower is expressly fixed or mentioned at the marriage ceremony, the law confers the right of dower upon the wife as a necessary effect of marriage. To use the language of the *Hedaya*, 'the payment of dower is enjoined by the law merely as a token of respect for its object (the woman), wherefore the mention of it is not absolutely essential to the validity of a marriage; and, for the same reason, a marriage is also valid, although the man were to engage in the contract

> on the special condition that there should be no dower.'—(Hamilton's *Hedaya* by Grady, p. 44). Even after the marriage the amount of dower may be increased by the husband during coverture (Baillie's Digest, p. 111).[50] [emphasis added]

Asaf A.A. Fyzee, an eminent author on Muslim law has dedicated his book, *Cases in the Muhammadan Law of India, Pakistan and Bangladesh*[51]' to the memory of Justice Syed Mahmood. It reads, 'To the Memory of Justice Syed Mahmood Master of Law and Master of Language.'

An Arabic maxim *al yaqin la yazul bilshakk* meaning 'certainty is not overridden by doubt' was introduced to the legal world by Justice Mahmood through his judgment in the *Mazhar Ali v. Budh Singh case.*[52] This is Mahmood's yet another masterpiece that clarified the position of law on missing persons. The sticking point in the case was the purported conflict between the general law (Indian Evidence Act) and the personal law of Muhammadans. The principal question before the full bench comprising Chief Justice William Comer Pethram, Justice Oldfield, Justice Brodhurst, Justice Duthoit and Justice Syed Mahmood was the following:

> Does the rule contained in Section 108 of the Evidence Act govern the case of a Muhammadan who has been missing for more than seven years, in cases to which, under the provisions of Section 24 of the Civil Courts Act, the Muhammadan Law is applicable?[53]

Under the British system of administration of justice, according to the Civil Courts Act of 1871, persons belonging to the Muhammadan and Hindu religions were given the right to be governed in the matters therein enumerated (succession, inheritance, marriage, or caste—or any religious usage or institution) by their own personal law; however, issues other than those were to be dealt with under the general law.

Justice Mahmood observed that since the issue of missing persons is not related to the laws of succession, inheritance, marriage or caste, or any religious usage or institution, it therefore did not qualify to be covered under the personal law. Hence, the general law—or Indian Evidence Act, 1872—would be applicable to this case.

Relying on original sources and authorities on Muhammadan law, as well as its history tracing back to the time of Prophet Muhammad (P.B.U.H.) and the Caliphate period, he studied the evolution of the concept of *istis-hab*, a system of jurisprudence born out of the exigencies of administration. Elucidating the concept, he observed:

> It is a matter of the history of Muhammadan Law that when the Republic founded by the Prophet became an empire under the Khalifas of Baghdad, *the exigencies of administration necessitated the establishment of Courts of Justice, for decision of disputes, and it was about that time that the jurists and doctors of the law endeavoured to frame a system of jurisprudence by supporting it with reasons deduced from those logical methods which the Arabian*

*schoolmen had borrowed from the ancient philosophers of Greece*. It was in consequence of this that the earliest systematised text books of Muhammadan jurisprudence were written, and by the concurrence of generations of jurists, principles and maxims were formulated and accepted as guides for judicial decision. Among the maxims which were thus established is the maxim, '*Certainty is not overridden by doubt*',(1) which, says the author of the *Ashbah*, the most celebrated treatise on maxims of Muhammadan Law, 'has been explained by some doctors to mean that the requisitions of certainty are not removed by doubt.'(2) The author goes on to say: 'In this maxim are included various rules, one of which is, that original condition is continuance of what was in the same state as it was.'(3) This rule, which I have literally translated, is technically called *istis-hab*, and it is thus dealt with by the same author under the maxim which I have just cited. 'The second benefit,' says the author, 'derived from the maxim relates to *istis-hab*, which means (as in the Tahrir) that a thing ascertained exists till there is probability of its extinction. There is a difference of opinion whether the rule can be employed as an argument by a claimant. Some hold that it is an absolute argument, while many altogether deny its efficacy. But the three profound doctors, Abu-Zaid, Shamsul-Aimma, and Fakhrul-Islam Bazdawi, hold that the rule may be employed as an argument in defence but not in attack (that is, in resisting a claim but not in seeking a right), and this doctrine has been generally accepted by

> the lawyers. . . . Another outcome of the maxim is that a missing person neither inherits nor is he inherited from.'(4) Fakhrul-Islam Bazdawi (to whom the author of the Ashbab has referred), in his celebrated book entitled the *Principles of Jurisprudence* has treated the rule in the chapter on analogical presumptions in these words: 'But employing *istis-hab-alhal* (continuance of condition) as an argument is correct according to Shafei, and this applies to all matters the necessity whereof is established by reason, and then doubt arises as to the discontinuance of those matters. In such cases the rule of *istis-hab* holds good, so that it may be used against the opposite party. And according to us it cannot be an argument of proof on behalf of a claimant, but an argument in defence; and on this (principle) are grounded the doctrines of our doctors for example, the life of a missing person'.[54] [emphasis added]

The judgment stands out for its extensive research on works of a wide range of jurists such as Abu-Zaid, Shamsul-Aimma, Fakhrul-Islam Bazdawi, Abu Yusuf, Imam Abubakar Muhammad Ibn-ul-Fazl, Sadrul-Shahid, Hasan-ibn-i-ziad, Abu Hanifa, Imam Malik, Shaikh Imam Abubakr Muhammad Ibn-i-Bami and authorities on Muslim law including *Ashbah*, *Hedaya*, *Khulasa*, *Fatwa-i-Alamgiri* and *Zaul Faraiz Sirajiya*.

But it was not only in Muhammadan law that Mahmood had his metier. His judicial aptitude sparkled in other areas of law as well.

## Hindu Law Judgments

While it is considerably evident that Mahmood's proficiency in Arabic immensely contributed to catapulting his standing in Muslim law akin to a 'school of thought' in himself, one would naturally assume that his knowledge of Hindu law would not be as formidable. However, and astonishingly so, from a glance of his judgments on Hindu law, his knowledge of original texts and scriptures comes out as markedly vast.

Mahmood's judgment in *Janki v. Nand Ram*[55] is recognised as a milestone for ushering in a new ground for providing maintenance to widows covering situations not otherwise conceived under the Hindu law. In this case, Justice Mahmood protected the widow of a predeceased son by holding that she was entitled to maintenance from her husband's brother, who had inherited the self-acquired property of his father. Mahmood's stance was based on his conviction that where the language of law is equivocal, the interpretation that benefits the weak and indigent should be preferred by the courts. Through this judgment, he successfully laid down the grounds for extension of 'moral obligations' into 'legal obligations' for maintenance of a Hindu widow.

Professor Virendra Singh Rekhi, an eminent scholar of law from AMU, described Mahmood's judgment as a 'revolution in miniature exhibiting forthright activism.'[56]

The view considered by Justice Mahmood in *Binda v. Kaunsilia and another*[57] was instrumental in drawing the legislative framework of the Hindu

Marriage Act, 1955—the modern codified Hindu law governing marriage and divorce of the Hindus.

His decision is believed to have opened new vistas for the rights of Hindu wives. In cases where the wife withdrew from the company of the husband because of being subjected to cruelty, Justice Mahmood recognised it as a sufficient cause for refusing the plea of the husband for cohabitation with his wife. He affirmed the views of the Privy Council in an earlier case which stated that even a Hindu husband could be refused the help of the court in restitution if his conduct was not blameless, and that suitable conditions could be imposed by the court if it granted a decree of restitution.[58]

This view taken by him has now received statutory recognition under the Hindu Marriage Act, 1955.

In arriving at his view, Justice Mahmood relied on his readings from the original ancient Hindu texts of *Manu,*[59] *Harita*[60] *and Lichita.*[61] From a holistic reading of these texts, he concluded that they are not mere moral precepts but rules of law creating legal rights and duties between the husband and wife.

Resorting to a balanced view on the remedy for the restitution of conjugal rights,[62] he observed that it could be availed by either spouse whose company has been abandoned by the other without any reasonable justification.

The impact of Justice Mahmood's judgment in *Indar Kaur v. Lalta Prasad Singh*[63] on the 'property rights of a Hindu widow' has been recorded as progressively affirmative.

The ruling had the effect of extending the rights of a Hindu widow in respect of her share in her deceased husband's immovable property and her power of alienation thereof. The issue in this case pertained to the limitations on the power of a Hindu widow in respect of disposal of immovable property inherited upon the death of her husband.

A harmonious reading of the ancient Hindu text (shastras) and principles of equity (doctrine of legal necessity) led Justice Mahmood to reading down the limitation on the power of Hindu widow, to alienate immovable property inherited by her upon the death of her husband.

Justice Mahmood observed that the original shastras had no such provision of limitation. He further added:

> But this extension of the original doctrine seems to have arisen from the exigencies of modern life rather than the precepts of Hindu Law, and to have originated in the principles of equity, which could not be disregarded in administering an ancient law, and in adapting its behests to the present conditions of life in British India. It is necessary to point out this distinction, because the expression 'legal necessity' does not appear to be a term of Hindu Law, and has not, so far as I am aware, been exhaustively defined by any authentic decision. It is only by instances that an idea of what amounts to legal necessity can be gathered from the Hindu Law, and the numerous decisions to be found in the law reports.[64]

His judgments in *Lekhraj Singh v. Ganga Sahai*[65] and *Beni Prasad v. Hardai Bibi and Others*[66] are watershed on adoption under Hindu law, as they eased the restrictions on the adoption of sons. He found support for his interpretation from Hindu religious texts.

He drew on his profound knowledge of Sanskrit while examining the original texts from Mayukha and Manu and pointed out inaccuracies in the translation by Mandalik as the latter had translated not the original texts of Sage Vasishtha but a reading of the Mayukha with emendations. In reference to the dharma shastra of Sage Yajnavalkya, he studied Vijneshwara and discovered inadequacies in the work of Colebrooke, and therefore, took the aid of the original text of Nandapandita and compared it with Saunaka texts in *Dattaka Mimansa*.

His following observation is noteworthy:

> *I hold that such restrictions as are indicated in the texts upon the adoption of an only son are merely religious and moral as distinguished from legal;* that they amount to moral or religious admonitions relating to the choice or selection of an only son for purposes of adoption as a matter resting between the giver and the taker; that as such admonitions they do not in law vitiate any one of the three capacities which I have held are essential to the legal validity of Hindu adoption. And it follows, therefore, that the doctrine of factum valet[67] applies to this case.[68] [emphasis added]

## Other Cases

The decision in *Kandhiya Lal v. Chandar*[69] is another fine dissenting judgment of Mahmood on an issue lying at the point of intersection between the law of contracts (English law) and the Hindu law of inheritance (native law).

The issue before the court related to the competence of a shareholder (part owner) to sue for the recovery of the entire amount due on the bond owned by several shareholders. In contractual terms, it refers to the question of payment *in solido or* amount payable in solidity— the whole amount of debt due to different creditors can be recovered by one creditor under the law.

He ruled that a shareholder could not sue for more than his share in the bond. Specifically, here the subject matter of the contract is the entire sum or *in solido*, no one party can bring a separate action for his share. In other words, if the right to realise the money has devolved in specific shares upon the heirs of the deceased, each of such heirs cannot maintain a separate suit for the recovery of his share, if the intention is to pay only one sum *in solido*.

Mahmood relied on the works of Story, Pothier and Demolombe on contract and Domat on civil law. He creatively outlined the role of law in society, while juxtaposing native rules of inheritance with European systems.

> As to the advisability of applying the rules of jurisprudence to this country, I have long entertained the opinion that jurisprudence, being a science, is and must be applicable to all conditions of life where society has sufficiently advanced to render the introduction of the rules of law necessary for defining rights and deciding disputes; and *I cannot help feeling that the complications which the Hindu*

> *and the Muhammadan Law of inheritance produce in connection with the devolution of rights are not greater than those produced by the laws of Europe, where the principles of jurisprudence are of course kept in view in administering justice.*[70] [emphasis added]

Justice Mahmood has in his well-recorded dissent in the judgment of *Chittor Mal v. Shib Lal*[71] laid to rest a controversy on an open question of law. The question was related to the scope of law governing a key aspect of agricultural lands in India. Specifically, he is credited for protesting wholesale transplantation of English law to Indian conditions as unreasonable.

Furthermore, he extended the scope of the doctrine of salvage[72] by bringing it within the realms of equity. Through this blend, he devised an instrument to dispense justice between the co-sharers of the agricultural lands in situations where one sharer has cleared the arrears of revenue due on the other co-sharers.

The case related to payment of revenue due on an agricultural land that was jointly owned by multiple sharers. His judgment had the effect of providing relief to one co-sharer who had paid the full amount of revenue due on the entire land. Infusing the principles of equity in such situations led Justice Mahmood to protect the interest of the co-sharer (who paid the entire amount) against that of the other co-sharers (on whom arrears were due).

The judgment is also known for Mahmood's impressions on the 'duties of a judge' in the Indian context—especially by juxtaposing the functions of a judge with a legislator. He observed:

> It is perfectly true that in dealing questions not covered by express legislative provisions, the judge must not forget that he is a judge and not a legislator. But it is equally true that a judge sitting in one country is not to administer the laws of another country.[73]

Justice Mahmood is also acknowledged for widening the scope of procedural laws.[74] In the case of *Narsingh Das v. Mangal Dubey and others*,[75] he observed:

> . . . the courts are not to act upon the principles that every procedure is to be taken as prohibited unless it is expressly provided for by the Code, but on the converse, principles that every procedure is to be understood as permissible till it is shown to be prohibited by the law.[76]

His dissenting opinion in *Lutfunnissa v. Jamiatunnissa*[77] holds significance even today in answering questions on the applicability of a cardinal doctrine of civil law—doctrine of res judicata. The doctrine of res judicata enunciates that a matter which has been adjudicated by a competent court cannot be pursued again by the same parties in another court.

The question before the full bench of the court was:

> Can a defendant file objections under Section 561 of the Civil Procedure Code to, or appeal under Section 540 from, a decree, which upon the face of it dismisses the plaintiff's claim in general terms, and does not record any adverse finding or declaration in respect of such defendant?

To put it simply, the question before the court can be divided into two parts:

1. Whether the findings of the district court on the issues before it constituted merely an 'obiter dictum'[78] or would be binding upon the defendant so as to operate as res judicata?
2. Whether the appeal by the defendant against the judgment of the district court was maintainable before the high court?

Answering the questions in the affirmative, Justice Mahmood respectfully distanced himself from the majority opinion. To address the first question, he held that the doctrine of res judicata bars the reagitation of issues just as it bars the trial of suits. In the instant case, the matter directly and substantially in issue between the parties was adjudicated upon by the first court. Therefore, the finding upon the issue was not a mere obiter dictum but was binding upon the defendant, so as to operate as res judicata.

Illustrating the reason behind the maxim *nemo debet bis vexari pro eadem causa* (no person should be twice vexed for the same cause), he pointed out that it was intended to mitigate the harassment of litigants. He wrote:

> The reason of the maxim *Nemo debet bis vexari pro eadem causa* seems to me to apply as much to the trial of issues as to the trial of suits, for in either case the harassment to litigants would be similar if matters could be re-agitated after having been once duly adjudicated upon.[79]

As regards the second question—on the maintainability of the appeal—he held that whatever has the force of res judicata is necessarily appealable.

Mahmood's opinion minimised the harassment of litigants by limiting the scope for reagitation of issues already adjudicated upon.

The *Madras Law Journal* in 1930 commented as follows on his decision:

> Mr. Justice Mahmood's view on res judicata as to issues in *Jamaitunnissa v. Lutfunnissa* is worth considering even today, though he was in the minority and though his point of view has not received acceptance. The reputation of the Allahabad High Court is not very high and that is due to the fact that besides Justice Mahmood there is no outstanding personality of striking ability among the Judges of that Court that one could think of.[80]

His conviction that technical defects ought not to impinge upon the substantive rights of litigants were further amplified in his judgment in *Muhammad Salim v. Nabian Bibi and Others,*[81] wherein he expanded on the thread he laid down in *Lutfunnissa v. Jamiatunnissa*—on the operation of the doctrine of res judicata.

Here, a suit filed for obtaining the possession of property under a sale deed was dismissed on technical grounds of undervaluation and misjoinder of parties (the wrong party is made a party to the suit). The plaintiff appellant had failed to deposit the additional court fees (payable when the suit property is not correctly valued;

an amount lower than duly payable is paid as the court fees) within due time as mandated under Section 10 of the Court-Fees Act. Subsequently, the plaintiff filed another plaint seeking the same remedy from the court in respect to the same suit property. It was contended on behalf of the respondents that the second suit was barred *in limine* according to the doctrine of res judicata. The lower court dismissed the suit without going into the merits of the case.

Justice Mahmood heard the case in appeal. The two questions framed in appeal were: first, whether the dismissal of the plaintiff's former suit under Section 10 of the Court-Fees Act can be regarded as res judicata barring the present action; and second, whether the dismissal of a suit for misjoinder would have any such effect. To be specific, it was to be determined whether the dismissal of the suit *ba haisiyat maujuda*—that is, in the form in which it was brought afresh—which occurs in the Munsif's order in the former suit dated the 9 November 1872 has any bearing upon the question.

Remanding the case to the court of first instance by setting aside the decrees of both the lower courts, Mahmood observed:

> But, as I have already said, that decree disposed of the suit upon the ground of purely technical defects, which in a just juridical sense cannot be regarded as a final adjudication upon the rights of the parties, so as to furnish a basis for application of the plea known in the Roman law under the name of exceptio rei judicata, which is the foundation

> of the rule incorporated in s. 13 of our own Civil Procedure Code. And interpreting that section as I do, I adopt the language used by the learned Judges of the Madras High Court in *Saikappa Chetti v. Hani Kulandapuri Nachiyar*, (3 M.H.C.R. 84) when I say that to conclude a plaintiff by a plea of res judicata, it is not sufficient to show that there was a former suit between the same parties, for the same matter, upon the same cause of action. It is necessary also to show that there was a decision finally granting or withholding the relief sought.[82]

With regard to the interpretation of Section 10 of the Court-Fees Act and dismissal of suit under it as a bar to the subsequent suit, he ruled the following:

> I wish to say in the first place is that the object of these provisions, as indeed of the whole Act, is to lay down rules for the collection of one form of taxation, and this I regard to be the scope of the enactment, though it contains no preamble at all, I hold it as a fundamental rule of construction that statutes which impose pecuniary burdens, or encroach, upon the rights of the subject, or qualify those rights must be construed strictly. The rule applies with especial force to such provisions as provide a penalty, whatever its nature may be. These rules which are applied by Courts of Justice in England to Acts of Parliament are too well recognised to require any citation of authorities, and I hold that they are in the main applicable to the interpretation of the enactments of the Indian Legislature. This being

> so, I am of opinion that the dismissal of a suit under s. 10 of the Court Fees Act is intended to be simply a penal clause to enforce the collection of the court-fees, and that if such dismissal is sought to operate as a plea barring a fresh action *in limine* as res judicata, we must look elsewhere in the statute book.[83]

Syed Mahmood's marvellous dissent in *Gopal Pandey v. Parsottam Das*[84] explains with clarity a nuanced point of law—how provisions of a procedural character create substantive rights. The ruling is distinctive for its comparative study of the Indian and Roman law on transfer of property. He explained the nature of the right of occupancy by drawing upon the analogy of Roman jurisprudence *Nuda Proprietas*[85] *and Emphytusis.*[86]

To prove that provisions of a procedural character had really created substantive rights, he analysed the nature of right that emanated in the immovable property to its occupancy tenant. Under the rent law that prevailed in the NWP, a tenant acquired the right of occupancy merely by virtue of occupying or cultivating land continually for a period of 12 years. Such continual occupation created the effect of conferring benefits on the tenant. In other words, although the landlord continued to be the owner of the land, the tenant acquired a right to occupy and cultivate the soil wholly—as long as he did not contravene the provisions of the relevant rent control legislation. In respect of the occupancy right of the tenant so created, Justice Mahmood observed that although such rights appear to fall in the province of procedure or adjective law on the subject of recovery of rent, in reality, this has the effect of creating a substantive right in favour of the tenant.

He observed that the occupancy right runs with the land, and the life duration of the tenant is immaterial to it. He held the right of occupancy to be not only transferable and inheritable but also a right in *rem*—a right that is enforceable against the world.

To lend credence to his viewpoint, he relied on noted jurists John Austin and Holland:

> The right no doubt falls far short of absolute ownership or dominion defined by Austin to be a 'right over a determinate thing indefinite in point of user, unrestricted in point of disposition, and unlimited in point of duration'. But 'one or more of the subordinate elements of ownership, such as a right of possession or user, may be granted out while the residuary right of ownership—called by the Romans nuda proprietor—remains unimpaired [sic]. The elements of the right which may thus be disposed of without interference with the right itself—in other words, which may be granted to one person over an object of which another continues to be the owner–are known *as jura in re alien*a'—(Holland on Jurisprudence[sic], p. 144.) Thus *jura in re aliena* are such of the rights in rem, availing against the world at large, as are acquired over and in the absolute ownership or dominion of another person in whom the ownership still continues. Among such rights was a right known to Roman jurisprudence as *emphyteusis*, which has been defined to be 'the right of a person who was not the owner of a piece of land,

> to use it as his own in perpetuity, subject to forfeiture on non-payment of a fixed rent, and on certain other contingencies'.[87]

The Law Commission of India, an advisory body to the Government of India on legal reforms, has in its 70th Report[88] referred to the observation of Justice Syed Mahmood in *Mata Din Kasodhan v. Kazim Hussain*[89] in recommending a wider interpretation of the term 'property'. He approved the definition of *property* given by *Wharton's Law Lexicon*: 'The highest right a man can have to anything, being used for that right—as to lands or tenements, goods or chattels, which does not depend on another's courtesy.'[90]

On the issue of transferability of property, he further observed that, 'Section 6 of the Transfer of Property Act, 1882 in making exceptions to transferability, must be understood to use the term 'property' in its widest and most generic legal sense, for otherwise the exceptions would be wholly unnecessary.'

The observations made by him in the case of *Palakhdhari Singh v. The Collector of Gorakhpur and Others*[91] find mention in the 69th Law Commission Report[92] on the Indian Evidence Act, 1872 in reference to the admissibility of the judgments as evidence. The following observation of Justice Mahmood was quoted by the commission:

> I know enough of that system to feel sure that it does not permit admissibility of the evidence furnished

> by judicial adjudications except where such previous adjudication operates either as res judicata or relates to a custom or right of public nature. Judgments of that character cannot of course, operate as res judicata in English system of law or any other unless they are between the same parties or those whom they represent.[93]

Justice Mahmood's rulings as discussed above aptly encapsulate his judicial metier. They have been much cited and relied upon by the Supreme Court of India and several different high courts in their various decisions, instances of which are perhaps too copious to be reproduced here.

That is not all though. Over the years, Justice Mahmood's interpretations have acquired transnationality by being referred to by courts in foreign jurisdictions. The higher judiciary of Pakistan, Bangladesh, Malaysia, Singapore, Kenya and others have taken recourse to his judgments to tailor judicial interpretations in their legal systems. For instance, *Queen Empress v. Pohpi*, *Chittor Mal v. Shib Lal*, *Ishri v. Gopal Saran*, *Muhammad Allahadad Khan v. Muhammad Ismail Khan* have been referred to in Pakistan,[94] *Gobind Dayal v. Inayatullah* in Bangladesh,[95] *Palakdhari Singh v. The Collector of Gorakhpur and Others* in Malaysia,[96] *Mazhar Ali v. Budh Singh* in Kenya,[97] to name a few.

Hindustan Times
FIRST VOICE. LAST WORD.

# From the 19th century, the story of a dissenting judge and colonialism

At a time when courage has become rare, one has to look up to those who stood for dissent in the colonial era.

Syed Mahmood, son of the great social reformer of 19th century India, Sir Syed Ahmed Khan, was the perhaps first judge to espouse the cause of judicial freedom. He was born on May 24 in 1850.

Mahmood made history during his six-year stint as a judge of the Allahabad High Court (HC) from 1887 to 1893, which was the highest position a "native" could hold in the British Government of India.

He was the first Indian Muslim and the first north Indian to be appointed to any HC in India, besides being the first non-European member of the Allahabad Bar.

Mohammad Nasir

From the age of 32 in 1882, he officiated as a judge of Allahabad HC thrice, before eventually becoming permanent in 1887.

As a judge, Mahmood stood out for demonstrating judicial integrity through dissent.

Even while he was still only a temporary judge of the Allahabad HC, he wrote dissenting judgments with vigour and fearlessness, and put humanity at the centre of his judicial universe, a digression from the purely legalistic approach of earlier judges.

In his famous dissenting judgment in Queen Empress vs Phopi, he recognised "fair trial" as an essential part of the criminal justice system, in defiance of the then colonial law, to protect the rights of the accused in situations where they were neither present in person before the court nor represented by a lawyer.

Similarly, in Queen Empress vs Babulal, his dissent put checks on torture of prisoners for extraction of confessions under the colonial evidence law.

Thereafter, the chief justice of Allahabad HC, Sir John Edge, stopped assigning Mahmood criminal cases. Eventually, this hostility with Chief Justice Edge culminated in Mahmood's resignation from judgeship in 1893. As a truly independent judge, he simply could not accept judgeship being dependant on the frowns and smiles of the British.

Sir Syed, his father, saw it as a spiteful act of "Englishmen robbing Indian civil servants of their self-respect", but was proud his son had the courage to stand up to the British.

Tej Bahadur Sapru, a prominent Indian freedom fighter who helped in drafting the Indian Constitution, termed the episode a "public calamity".

Imagine those days of the last quarter of the 19th century when Justice Mahmood was the only Indian among British judges.

As an Indian judge of standing in colonial India, he perhaps exemplified the burden of double consciousness — having to think of as an Indian judge in British India.

As a son of India with a judicial aptitude far ahead of his time, many of his dissents were later accepted by the courts, and continue to be the law of the land.

He was quoted by the Supreme Court (SC) of India in the Shayara Bano judgment abolishing the practice of triple *talaq*; and recently, in 2020, SC in Raghunath vs Radha Mohan, quoted with approval his judgment on the Muslim law of pre-emption.

While Mahmood is most reputed for his *metier* in Muslim law, his judicial scholarship sparkled in other areas of law as well, leavened by his vintage quest for a reason to confront orthodoxy and dogma.

His pronouncements on Hindu Law not only widened the grounds for Hindu widows for claiming maintenance, but were also useful in drawing the legislative framework of the Hindu Marriage Act, 1955 — the modern codified Hindu law governing marriage and divorce.

The enduring light of Mahmood shines from the intellectual integrity he never let go of in moments of conflict.

To the Indian legal fraternity, he will inspire us to learn deeply, think clearly and most crucially, never be afraid, when it is time to speak.

*Mohammad Nasir is an assistant professor of law at Aligarh Muslim University*
*The views expressed are personal*

*Hindustan Times op-ed tribute to Justice Syed Mahmood on his birth anniversary 24 May 2021*

# 5

# Engagements after Resignation from Judgeship and Last Days

After his resignation as a judge, Mahmood measured up to his father's expectations by actively engaging in the academic and administrative affairs of MAO College. In 1894, he sold his palatial house in Allahabad to Raja Premanand of Moradabad, a judge of Shahjahanpur, from whom it was bought in the year 1900 by Pandit Motilal Nehru, who was then a prominent lawyer at Allahabad and later became president of the Congress party. The house is now known as Anand Bhavan, also popularly called Swaraj Bhavan.

*Swaraj Bhavan, the residence of Justice Mahmood at Allahabad. It was later bought by Pandit Motilal Nehru.*

## Lectures at Educational Conference

Mahmood also enthusiastically participated in the proceedings of the All India Muhammadan Educational Conference, a body founded by Sir Syed Ahmad Khan in 1886 at Aligarh, with the primary objective to keep Muslims tethered to modern education. Originally established as the 'All India Muhammadan Educational Congress', it was later renamed 'All India Muhammadan Educational Conference', in order to end speculations that it was formed to oppose the Indian National Congress. Years later, at the 36th annual meeting of the conference in 1923, the name was again changed to 'All India Muslim Educational Conference'—a name it has retained till date.

At the invitation of the All India Muhammadan Educational Conference, Mahmood presented a series of enlightening lectures in the conferences of 1893 and 1894 at Aligarh, on the theme 'Rise, Development, Progress, and Present Condition of English Education in India with Special Reference to the Muhammadans'. The sessions were held at the central hall of MAO College with around 600 delegates from all over India in attendance.

The literature on the history of British India was loaded with the content on public administration, legislations, treaties and the battles fought, but there was a dearth of literature on the history of English education, its introduction and development during the British Raj, which could be used as a model book for the promotion of education in India. While researching for his talks, Mahmood identified this gap in data on English education and its contribution in shaping the discourse and thought processes of Indians. The lectures were widely appreciated for the comprehensive and convincing evidence on the educational policies of the government, touching upon almost all the aspects of its organisation and administration.

To expand on the thread laid down in his initial lectures, he was again invited to the subsequent session to speak on 'The Present Rate of Progress of English Education among the Muhammadans and their Future Prospects'.

Mahmood spoke at length on the importance of English education along with oriental education for the holistic development of Muslims, both as individuals and as a community. Under the existing British rule, it became critical to blend traditional oriental learning with advanced English education which, in his view, will be a pivot for their growth, especially in higher echelons. He opined:

> It has never been the crying complaint of the Muhammadans that they have been backward either in vernacular or primary education or even in the higher kind of education of the oriental type. A knowledge of the Muhammadan vernacular has always been prevalent among that community, and the *Maktabs* or primary schools teaching the Koran and elements of Persian and Arabic, are scattered all over the country, and the higher grades of Muhammadan learning are still taught and cultivated by eminent Maulvis, here and there, who charge no fees and devote their lives to advancing learning from motives of piety and religion. In respect of the elementary stages of English education, also, the Muhammadans have during recent years made a satisfactory advance; but such education is not sufficiently pursued further by them up, to the higher grades of English standards, and falls far short of meeting the social, economical, and political needs

> of their population under the exigencies of the British Rule. *For any tangible social, economical and political effects on a community, the spread of higher English education is necessary in India, whilst it is obvious that for all the higher walks of life under the British Rule a competent knowledge of the English language is now indispensable.*[1] [emphasis added]

This is not to be understood as Mahmood's preference for English education at the cost of traditional learning. In fact, in the same conference, he is believed to have supported the resolution favouring the Nadwatul Uloom—an emerging organisation of learned scholars, who had met at Cawanpore a few days earlier.[2]

Nadwatul Uloom was established in 1893 by a group of Muslim scholars as a council to reform the prevalent educational system, and to eliminate the differences among Muslim groups on different religious issues. The Nadwatul Uloom established under its umbrella an academic institution—Darul Uloom Nadwatul Ulama—which has now emerged as one of the most premier institutions of Islamic theological studies in India.

Mahmood's lectures at the conferences comprised an in-depth analysis of the data and statistics available in the government reports and surveys and his own experiences in civil services, judiciary, legislation and academia. Portraying the grim condition of education amongst the Muslims in India, he enjoined the community to introspect and identify their own shortcomings. He attributed their educational backwardness to apathy and reluctance to read beyond their own literature and oriental subjects. Moreover, the course of instruction Muslims followed was highlighted as an impediment.

Believing that education would be a catalyst in enabling them to optimally utilise opportunities like their Hindu brothers, he drew a healthy comparison between the two communities. He said:

> Such feelings of aversion towards English education entertained by the Muhammadan [sic], and evinced so early as 1835, stand in strong contrast to the attitude of the Hindu community, who, as has been shown, had zealously proved their desire to acquire a knowledge of the English language, literature, sciences, by founding the Anglo-Indian College, so far back as 1816, and the memorial which had been presented on their behalf by Raja Ram Mohan Roy to Lord Amherst, the then Governor-General of India. The difference between the sentiments of the two communities towards English education is the real key to the reasons of the vast disparity of progress in English education which the two nationalities have respectively made. The effects of this disparity have been most baneful to the interests of British India in general, and the Mahomedan community in particular, and those effects have not yet disappeared.[3]

To demonstrate the progress of education in the two dominant communities in India—Hindus and Muslims—Mahmood made a tabular representation statistically comparing their representation in various branches of learning in Indian universities. The data derived was truly comprehensive, covering the records of 36 years from 1858 to 1893, both inclusive. The table has been reproduced below.

*TABLE 5.1. Comparative statistics of higher English education in British India among Hindus and Muhammadans for 36 years (1858–1893)*

| *Subjects* | *Arts* | | *Law* | | *Medicine and surgery* | | *Engineering* | | *Total* | | |
|---|---|---|---|---|---|---|---|---|---|---|---|
| | *Hindus* | *Muhammadans* | *Hindus* | *Muhammadans* | *Hindus* | *Muhammadans* | *Hindus* | *Muhammadans* | *Hindus* | *Muhammadans* | *Total* |
| Number of graduates | 9715 | 399 | 3537 | 110 | 1239 | 34 | 590 | 3 | 15081 | 546 | 15627 |
| Percentage of graduates | 96.1 | 3.9 | 96.98 | 3.02 | 97.13 | 2.87 | 99.5 | .5 | 96.5 | 3.5 | ... |
| Average number of graduates per year | 269.9 | 11.1 | 98.2 | 3 | 34.4 | .99 | 16.4 | 1 | 418.9 | 15.1 | 434.08 |
| Hindu and Muhammadan population of British India according to the census of 1881 | .... | .... | ... | ... | ... | ... | ... | ... | 14,48,75,315 | 4,51,27,033 | 19,00,02,348 |

| Percentage of Hindu and Muhammadan population of British India in 1881 | .... | .... | ... | ... | ... | ... | ... | ... | 76.25 | 23.75 | ... |
|---|---|---|---|---|---|---|---|---|---|---|---|
| Ratio of graduates according to the ratio Muhammadan: Hindu population | 96.1 | 29.9 | 96.98 | 30.2 | 97.13 | 30.3 | 99.5 | 31.0 | 96.5 | 30 | ... |
| Number of Muhammadan graduates according to the ratio Muhammadan: Hindu population | ... | 3,286 | ... | 1,475 | ... | 519 | ... | 161 | .... | 5,441 | ... |
| Actual number of Hindu and Muhammadan graduates | 9,715 | 399 | 3,537 | 110 | 1239 | 34 | 590 | 3 | 15,081 | 546 | 15,627 |
| Deficiency in the number of Muhammadan graduates | ... | 2,887 | ... | 1,365 | ... | 485 | .... | 158 | ... | 4,895 | ... |

Source: Mahmood, *A History of English Education in India*, 1895

This table has been extracted from Mahmood's, *A History of English Education in India,* which was largely based on the two lectures he delivered at the All India Muhammadan Educational Conference.

In his lectures, he also shed light on the inhibiting factors that vitiated harmony and cohesion between the Muslims and Britishers in India. He urged the Muslims to initiate dialogue and work for the socio-economic, educational and political betterment of themselves and the upcoming generations. For this, participation and adequate representation in the government was necessary.

While appreciating the role of the Aligarh Movement, as epitomised by MAO College and the All India Muhammadan Educational Conference, he felt the movement had geographical limitations in that it was largely confined to north and central India. He exhorted the All India Muhammadan Educational Conference to be a conduit in spreading the Aligarh Movement to remote areas that had not yet benefitted from its enlightenment. He said:

> The incessant efforts of Sir Syed Ahmad Khan and his fellow workers for spreading English education among Muhammadans, during more than a quarter of a century, have no doubt had beneficial effects on the Muhammadan population of that part of Upper India of which Aligarh, where the Muhammadan Anglo-Oriental College is situated, may be said to be the geographical centre, namely, the North-Western Provinces, Rohilkhand, Oudh, Behar, Punjab, and such portions of the Rajputana territories as are

> easily accessible by railways. But though the general effects of the educational movement, as represented by the Muhammadan Anglo-Oriental College and the Muhammadan Educational Conference, may have been felt far and wide, the Provinces included in the Presidencies of Madras and Bombay, as well as Bengal, Assam, and Burma, are so remote from the centre of the movement that its effects cannot fail to be very faint. [1]

The conference, therefore, concentrated on the spread of modern and scientific education among Muslims all over the country in a manner that the centrality of Aligarh in the educational movement was maintained. In such a backdrop, Mahmood's lectures were thereby an orientation programme for the activists of the conference, enabling them to propagate its mission.

Abdul Rashid Khan, author of *The All India Muslim Educational Conference: Its Contribution to the Cultural Development of Indian Muslims 1886-1947*, notes that Syed Mahmood sponsored the meals served to the delegates of the annual meeting of the All India Muhammadan Educational Conference held at Lucknow in 1887.[4]

## Mahmood's Book on History of English Education in India

These lectures formed the foundation for his magnum opus titled *A History of English Education in India: Its Rise, Development, Progress, Present Condition and*

*Prospects Being a Narrative of the Various Phases of Educational Policy and Measures Adopted under the British Rule from Its Beginning to the Present Period (1781–1893)*, published in 1895.

Outside many of his path-breaking judgments, Mahmood is known as a scholar for this work. The work illuminates his comprehensive research exhibited through statistical tables and detailed referencing. He collated data from official reports, parliamentary bluebooks, resolutions passed by the British government in India and recorded minutes of official meetings and programmes to produce a friendly comparative analysis of the progress of higher education in the Hindu and Muslim communities. The book contextualises the prevalent public opinion, facts and measures pertaining to education in India in the aftermath of the decline of the Mughal empire, and provides perspectives on the effect of education on the moral, social and political conditions of India.

The first part of the book evaluates the historical records from the inception of Indian universities of Calcutta, Madras and Bombay to 1893, including the advent of the East India Company and its pursuits. The next part appraises the status of English education amongst Indian Muslims and attempts to highlight its prospects.

The issue of the status of education of native females is conspicuous by its absence in the book. Mahmood was aware that the omission was glaring and adduced an explanation in the preface. He wrote:

> The English education, especially of the higher type, has made no perceptible progress among the Native female population of India. In Presidency towns a few native young ladies have pursued the University course, but their number is so infinitesimally small that it is intangible in any general calculation of the statistics of high English education, whilst this work is not concerned with Vernacular education.[5]

The book carries an interesting quote by Sir Richard Temple, a distinguished member of the Indian Civil Services, who later became the finance minister of British India, titled 'Female Education in Need of Benevolent Efforts' to accentuate the importance of western education. It states:

> Female education offers the greatest field now open to benevolent effort; in no other respect socially is there so much which needs doing, and which might practically be done. Doubtless some great result will ere long be attained, and that will affect mightily the coming generation. It is not likely that the Western education will at all extinguish the originality of mind which Indian women often have, notwithstanding the repressive influences of centuries. The flashes of ability and the sparks of character which have emanated from them—despite disadvantages which to European women would seem incredible—afford indications of what they may become hereafter, when their minds shall be freed.[6]

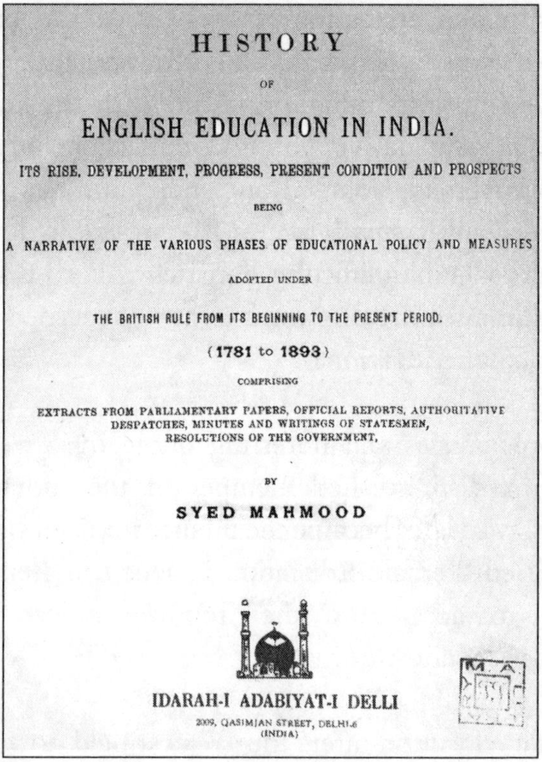

HISTORY

OF

ENGLISH EDUCATION IN INDIA.

ITS RISE, DEVELOPMENT, PROGRESS, PRESENT CONDITION AND PROSPECTS

BEING

A NARRATIVE OF THE VARIOUS PHASES OF EDUCATIONAL POLICY AND MEASURES

ADOPTED UNDER

THE BRITISH RULE FROM ITS BEGINNING TO THE PRESENT PERIOD.

(1781 to 1893)

COMPRISING

EXTRACTS FROM PARLIAMENTARY PAPERS, OFFICIAL REPORTS, AUTHORITATIVE DESPATCHES, MINUTES AND WRITINGS OF STATESMEN, RESOLUTIONS OF THE GOVERNMENT,

BY

SYED MAHMOOD

IDARAH-I ADABIYAT-I DELLI

2009, QASIMJAN STREET, DELHI-6

(INDIA)

*First edition of Syed Mahmood's book* A History of English Education in India

However, this book is not Mahmood's first and only intellectual foray on the subject of Muslim education. His first consequential incursion on the subject goes back to 1882—on the seat of the Indian Education Commission, also known as the Hunter Commission,[7] owing the name to its chairman, William Wilson Hunter, who was a member of the viceroy's council then. Constituted by the then Governor-General of India Lord Ripon in the backdrop of the revolt of 1857, it was the first education commission for India.

The commission was entrusted with the task of investigating the condition and development of education in India and to assess the existing defects. A part of its objectives was to examine the reasons behind the low enrolment ratio of Muslims in government schools and their under-representation in the government. It empanelled Sir Syed Ahmad Khan as a member for this exercise. However, since he was not well versed in English and faced considerable difficulty in pursuing the proceedings of the commission, he resigned from the membership. The *Aligarh Institute Gazette* of the period narrates that when Lord Lytton learnt of Sir Syed's resignation, he asked Sir Syed to persuade Syed Mahmood to become a member of the commission.[8] On Lord Lytton's persuasion, Mahmood agreed to take up the assignment.[9] His interest in scholarship centred on the education of Muslims encouraged him to take this opportunity to explore the root cause behind the backwardness of Muslims and their failure to acquire English education.

Mahmood's assistance to the commission is notable. During his tenure, 18 recommendations concerning the educational advancement and welfare of Muslims were made.[10] These are as follows:

1. The burden for the development and progress of Muslim education on the local, municipal and provincial funds should be considered lawful.
2. The management of the Islamic madrasas should be asked to increase the representation of secular subjects in those institutions.
3. Certain standards should be maintained in the primary schools of the Muslims.
4. In the primary and middle schools, except where the Muslims demand any other language, the medium of instruction should be Urdu.

5. Where the population of Muslims is considerable in proportion to the overall population, teaching of Urdu and Persian should be done in the primary and middle schools established and supported via public funds.
6. Where the language of the offices is not Urdu, it should be taught as an optional subject in those primary and middle schools that have been established for Muslims via public funds. Mathematics and account-keeping should be taught in Urdu.
7. People (Muslims) should be persuaded to pursue higher education because they need it very much.
8. Where necessary, Muslims should be awarded class-wise scholarships as prizes for the following:
   - In middle schools, after their success in primary schools. In high schools, after their success in middle schools.
   - In colleges, after their success in the entrance and First in Arts (F.A.) examinations (also known as Intermediate examinations).
9. In all kinds of schools established with public funds, some scholarships should be assigned specially for Muslim students. The number of such scholarships should be according to their strength in proportion to the total number of students.
10. In all such places where the income from the trusts (*auqaf*) is meant for the welfare of the Muslims and they are managed by the government, their income must be utilised only for the education of Muslims.
11. Where the *auqaf* trusts are managed privately or by certain groups of people, generous grants-in-aid should be given and people should be persuaded to

open schools and colleges for English education in accordance with the rules of the grants-in-aid.

12. Where necessary, normal schools should be established, or classes for the training of Muslim teachers should be organised.
13. In all Islamic schools (established by the *auqaf*) where the medium of instruction is Urdu, attempts should be made that all the teachers, as far as possible, should be Muslims.
14. School inspectors appointed from the Muslim community should inspect the Muslim schools more than the rules ask them to do.
15. The association for the progress of Muslims should be recognised and encouraged.
16. In the annual reports of public instruction, a special school should always be devoted to the education of Muslims.
17. The attention of the local government should be diverted to the factors that are considered at the time of giving employment to the educated Muslims and people of other communities.
18. The above-mentioned principles should also be applied to other communities, which are facing conditions similar to those of the Muslims.

As a commissioner, Mahmood cross-examined various witnesses who appeared before the commission, including his father, whose deposition runs in 32 printed pages. The two key propositions that became the subject of interchange between Mahmood and Sir Syed are as below:

1. Whether religious prejudices alone have kept Muhammadans aloof from English education or anything in their socio-political traditions had the same effect? In his reply, Sir Syed said, 'It may be briefly stated that the causes which have kept Muhammadans aloof from English education may be traced to four sources—their political traditions, social custom, religious beliefs and poverty.' He further argued on the need for Muslims to establish and fund educational institutions for their community, and not expect financial assistance from the government.
2. 'Why some British officials were opposed to the educational efforts by Indians?' was the other question, in response to which Sir Syed adduced 'mutual suspicion and lack of social intercourse' as the major reasons.[11]

Apart from Mahmood's lectures at the Muhammadan Educational Conference, the Hunter Commission report, too, shaped Mahmood's book. Sourced from the report are seven chapters of his book, namely, 'The Education Commission of 1882 and Some Important Facts and Statistics Collected by it in Regard to English Collegiate Education', 'The Grant-in-Aid System Inaugurated by the Education Despatch of 1854, and Considered by the Indian Education Commission', 'Views of the Indian Education Commission in Regard to the Withdrawal of the State from Higher Education', 'Moral Training and Religious Teaching in Colleges—Views of the Indian Education Commission—Mr Kashinath Trimbuk Telang's Dissentient Minute—Views of the Local Governments and the Decision of the Government of India upon the Subject', 'Measures Adopted by the Various

Local Governments as to Muhammadan Education under the Government of India's Resolution of 1871, as Stated in the Report of the Education Commission of 1882', 'Conclusions and Recommendations of the Education Commission of 1882, on the Subject of Muhammadan education—Reports of the Local Governments thereon—Views of the Government of India upon the Subject' and 'Expectations and Views of Eminent Statesmen Regarding the Political, Social, Moral and Religious Effects of English Education among the People of India—Opinions of the Education Commission of 1882 on the Subject'.

This work is still widely regarded as one of the most objective, insightful and in-depth analysis of the education system followed by the British in colonial India. In 2001, a book titled *English Education in Multilingual India* was published by the United Nations Educational Scientific and Cultural Organization (UNESCO) and contains extracts from this prolific book of Mahmood.[12] Mahmood transferred the copyright of this book to MAO College.[13] He did the same for his commentary on the Indian Evidence law titled *Sharah-e-Qanun Shahadat Majria Hind.*[14]

Mahmood also wrote two books on Muslim law, *Kitab al-Talaq* and *Kitab al-Shuf'ah*, that were published in 1897 in Urdu. *Kitab al-Talaq* is on the Muslim law of divorce, in the writing of which reliance was laid on *Sharh Majma al-Bahrain*, a notable work on Hanafi law on the subject. The other book, *Kitab al-Shuf'ah*, is a notable exposition on the Hanafi law on pre-emption, for which he drew on his reading of *Majma-ul-Bahrain*, *Fatawa Qazi Khan*, *Aini Shah Kanz*, *Hedaya Durr-e-Mukhtar* and *Sharh Wiqayah*.

کتاب الطلاق

از کتاب مذہب حنفی

شرح مجمع البحرین

حسب الارشاد آنریبل سید محمود

بیرسٹر ایٹ لا جعل ظله ممدودا

الہ آباد باہتمام احقر العباد

خواجہ مصلح الدین احمد

غفرله الاحد فی یوم

التناد

در مطبع مصلح المطابع واقع دہلی طبع شد

جولائی سنہ ۱۸۹۹ع

LYTTON LIBRARY ALIGARH MUSLIM UNIVERSITY

CHECKED Date..........

حق حقوق بذریعہ رجسٹری محفوظ ہیں

*Syed Mahmood's book* Kitab al-Talaq *(Law of Divorce)*

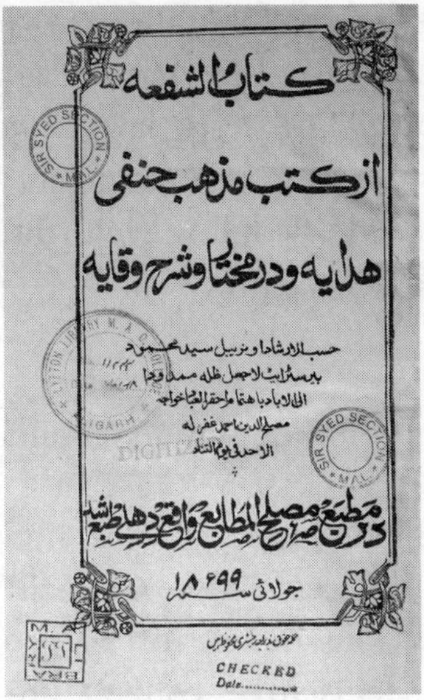
کتاب الشفعه
از کتب مذهب حنفی
هدایه و در مختار و شرح وقایه
در مطبع مصلح المطابع واقع دهلی طبع شد
جولائی سنه ۱۸۹۹
CHECKED
Date..........

*Syed Mahmood's book* Kitab al-Shuf'ah *(Law of Pre-emption)*

Besides his books, several newspapers and periodicals published in different parts of India—such as the *Englishman* from Calcutta (renamed later as the *The Statesman*), *Pioneer* and *Oudh Akhbar* from Lucknow, *Aligarh Institute Gazette* and *Tahzib ul-Akhlaq* from Aligarh—carried his opinion pieces in English and Urdu regularly.

Mahmood was also one of the founding members of the Council of Mohammedan Anglo-Oriental Defence Association of Upper India[15]—an organisation formed with the object to protect the political interests of Muslims by representing their views before the government.

In 1896, Mahmood returned to law practice before the Oudh Judicial Commissioner's Court at Lucknow. Satish Chandra Banerji joined him as a junior. He was well acquainted with Justice Mahmood as he joined

MAO College when his father, Avinash Chandra Banerji, was transferred to Aligarh as a judge of the small causes court. The young lawyer won Mahmood's heart with his acumen and assiduity. Unfortunately, owing to Mahmood's fledgling health due to alcoholism, he discontinued his law practice.

## Appointment to the Legislative Council

In January 1896, Mahmood was nominated to the NWP and Oudh Legislative Council[16] for a period of two years. The details of his contributions in the provincial legislative council are sparse. Alan M. Guenther from the Institute of Islamic Studies, McGill University has done admirable work to bring out details of Mahmood's nomination and subsequent involvement in the council.[17] He notes that the proposal to have Mahmood nominated to the Legislative Council was first contemplated while he was still a judge at the high court of Allahabad. The British desired to have a representation of an accomplished Muslim on the Provincial Council who was also a native of the province. However, the proposal waned as the British thought it would weaken the independence of the judiciary in the eyes of public, as Mahmood was on the high court bench then. Mahmood himself was averse to the idea of a member of the bench becoming a member of the legislature.

Mahmood, however, did harbour an aspiration to be on the seat of the legislature. He expressed it in his letter of resignation from the high court addressed to the chief secretary of the NWP and Oudh dated 9 September 1893. He wrote:

> If I had not been in Government employment I should most probably have offered myself as a candidate for the vacancy caused by my father's retirement from the local legislative Council and judging by almost innumerable letters of sympathy and good will which my father and I have received from my Mahomedan friends in all parts of India regarding my recent illness coupled as it was with the unfortunate friction with Sir John Edge, I venture to think that my nomination to the Council would have been very popular and it would have been most acceptable to me as I might prove useful to the Government in such legislation as the recent legislation regarding Village Tribunals, the proposals for which as you are aware was originated by me when Sir Alfred Lyall was Lieutenant Governor, and in which Sir Auckland Colvin was pleased to take a deep interest and which passed into law about the time when Sir Charles Crosthivante took charge of the Lieutenant Governor of these Provinces.[18]

He re-emphasised his wish again in the later part of the same letter, stating:

> In para 35 of this letter I took the liberty to say that had I not been in the Government service I should most probably have been a candidate for a seat in his Honour the Lieutenant Governor's Legislative Council, and I may now be permitted to say that as

> soon as my application for permission to retire is granted I may still seek to offer my humble services to the Government in the Department of Legislation . . . .[19]

After his resignation from the high court, the proposal to appoint him to the council was revisited a couple of years later, and his appointment was made on 23 January 1896. He was part of a sub-committee to review the draft Munsifs Bill. His prior works on judicial reform and administration, especially as a member of the judicial reforms commission in Hyderabad, enabled him to make significant contribution to the bill. This seems to be his only notable contribution in the council. His nominal contribution—or at least the sparse details available of them—appear surprising, given his robust opinions on the bills during the 1880s.

During this period, he regularly visited Aligarh where he resided at the house, presently known as 'Sir Syed House'.

## Persona Non Grata at MAO College

After the expiry of his term in the Legislative Council and withdrawal from law practice in Lucknow, he returned to Aligarh to aid his father in the running of MAO College. However, by this time, his intemperance had worsened considerably, which not only impaired his ability to discharge his responsibilities as the joint secretary of the college but also led to the deterioration of his relations with his father. Sir Syed, who breathed his last on 28 March 1898, found it difficult to live with Mahmood in the closing stages of his life. According to some accounts, he would drink and inconvenience his father ad nauseam with eccentricity till late in the night. The situation reached a nadir when his father, apparently in disgust, left the house to live in the adjoining area. Other accounts indicate that Syed Mahmood had turned him out of the house, leaving his father to lament, 'Alas! little did I know that Syed Mahmood would turn me out of the house at the end of my life, otherwise I would have built a small cottage for myself.'[20]

This version has been contradicted by other historians on Aligarh. Whatever may have been the case, Sir Syed was deeply grieved with the state of Mahmood's mental health in the final days of his life.

After the death of Sir Syed and as per the arrangements made in December 1889, Syed Mahmood assumed the office of honorary life secretary of MAO College. Corresponding with the worsening of his mental well-being, the political developments at the college posed a challenge to his position.

Mahmood's marginalisation from the affairs of MAO College is a dispiriting tale. Soon after assuming charge as the secretary of the college, differences emerged between him and associates of his father, who were trustees of the college—namely, Moulvi Samiullah Khan and Viqar-ul-Mulk.[21] They opposed his nomination as secretary, citing violation of the elective principle—Mahmood being the son of the predecessor-in-office.

While politicisation and opposition to Mahmood's central role in the affairs of MAO College by Sir Syed's associates gathered momentum after Sir Syed's death in 1898, a letter by Theodore Beck to Sir Syed dated 19 March 1896 suggests that a calibrated campaign to strip Mahmood of joint-secretaryship and the derailment of his possible future prospects for secretaryship had begun during Sir Syed's lifetime itself.[22] Apart from the elective principle, another point of difference that had emerged was regarding the entrustment of the management of the college to the European staff. Allegations on Mahmood of leniency in dealing with the Europeans intensified it further. Beck's letter alludes to this fact while mounting a spirited defence of Mahmood's indelible contribution to the college. Mahmood's mere presence, in Beck's estimation, was the reason for the harmonious coexistence of the European staff at the college with the natives in Aligarh. In him, the Europeans saw a just man—actuated by a sense of absolute justice in his dealings and discharge of his duties towards the college. Being a Cambridge man, he could understand the domestic life of Europeans and empathised with them, thereby mitigating any possible frictions.

Beck argued that being the principal of the college, he knew better than most about the selfless services rendered by Mahmood. In the same letter, he acknowledged Mahmood's utmost humility in not making a 'fuss or even talking about it'. As regards to monetary contribution, he said, '. . . he has probably given a larger portion of his income than any other living man in this college, though the sums have rarely appeared on any list of subscriptions. But this is the smallest part of his services.'[23]

Beck further mentioned that he not only owed his appointment to Mahmood but also accepted the offer based on the sense of security and confidence that Mahmood instilled in him. He revealed that ever since, Mahmood had been a confidant who actively engaged in the decision-making process of all important matters.

While Beck had initially defended Mahmood and considered him indispensable to the college, he, however, found Mahmood's conduct and inefficiency as the secretary of the college, indefensible. Mahmood's correspondence with him, as reproduced in *Syed Mahmood Papers*, also reveals the sad state of his mental faculty—circumlocution in explanation, lack of comprehension and misconstrued arguments. As the pitch for Mahmood's removal gathered momentum, Beck's patience with Mahmood had ended as brought out in his letter dated 22 July 1899 to Mohsin-ul-Mulk, a trustee of the college. An excerpt from the letter is shown below:

> I have made up my mind that as regards Mahmood, the Trustees will have to choose between me and him, for my health won't stand acting as a jailor of a lunatic asylum . . . my patience (with Mahmood) is now exhausted and I believe yours is too . . .[24]

Sounding alarm at Mahmood's vindictiveness proceeding with his drinking disease, he continued:

> . . . with the advance of his unfortunate disease (for I treat his drinking as an incurable disease) he is getting more vindictive . . . he takes the channel which his life long training makes easiest, i.e. he gives to law and brings law suits against people. He has been threatening this against many people for a long time . . . you and I and all the rest of us may be sued before long. . .[25]

Within 10 days of the letter, Mohsin-ul-Mulk moved a resolution in a meeting of the board of trustees held on 31 July 1899 that Syed Mahmood should resign from the office of secretary and accept the office of the life president of the college, a nominal position. Sensing that his position was becoming untenable, Mahmood conditionally agreed to accept the proposal, provided he was vested with the power to veto any proposal made by the secretary, which in his estimation, was not fit. The trustees did not accept the condition imposed, and on the persuasion of Mohsin-ul-Mulk, Mahmood resigned from the post and consequently, accepted the presidentship.[26]

*Syed Mahmood with Sir Syed and Mohsin-ul-Mulk, who succeeded Syed Mahmood as the secretary of MAO College*

After the death of Principal Theodore Beck, Professor Theodore Morison joined as the principal in October 1899. Soon after, he too faced difficulties while working in the presence of Mahmood, whose idiosyncrasies intensified, and his interferences in the working of the college became too frequent. Thereafter, in January 1900, the trustees, on the insistence of Morison, moved the resolution for the removal of Syed Mahmood from the office of president, citing his inability to discharge his duties due to mental imbalance and excessive interference in college affairs. Mahmood unsuccessfully challenged his removal before the lieutenant governor of NWP and Oudh. In October 1901, Syed Mahmood was named as the visitor to the college—a ceremonial post.[27]

## Final Days in Sitapur

Syed Mahmood spent the last three years of his life, until 1903, in Sitapur with his paternal cousin Syed Muhammad Ahmad, who had retired as a sub-judge in British India and settled in Sitapur. His move to locate to Sitapur was fuelled by the political developments at MAO College that led to his complete severance from its affairs, much to his chagrin.

In Sitapur, he drew subsistence from his love for literature, poetry, writing and law. His affable personality helped him forge a close bond with some well-known personalities in Sitapur including Maulana Hadi Ali Khan, Hakeem Syed Muhammad Sadiq, Moulvi Ahmad Hasan and Mirza Bahadur, amongst others. Their regular evening discussions were intense and revolved around subjects as varied as academics, law and religion. During his stay in Sitapur, his sister-in-law, Saeed-un-Nisa Begum,[28] nursed him with greatest sympathy and forbearance.

Interestingly, Mahmood in one of his letters touched upon the layout of his life plan. He wrote:

> Many years ago when I first began seriously to lay down definite plans for my future, I, following the example of one of my ancestors took ordinary human life to be the Psalmist's age of 70 years of which I allotted one third for educating myself, the second-third to earning a competence, and the remaining third to retired study authorship and devotion to matters of public utility, following in the steps of my father. I entered into the work of

> my profession in the twenty second years of my life and my actual service as a judge of the High Court being 7 years and 7 months (as I have shown in para 13 of a separate letter to your address which, I have prepared relating to my retirement) actual service of another period of 2 years and 5 months would entitle me to a pension of £ 800 per annum at a time of life when I should have completed two-thirds of my estimate of human life leaving me the remaining one-third of estimated human life for devotion to the objects which I have mentioned as my projected plans of life.[19]

In the outlined life plan of 70 years, his allusion to devoting the final third of his life in the footsteps of his father reveals his earnest desire to carry forward the legacy of his father at MAO College. However, destiny had other plans, for death, fuelled by his excessive alcoholism, knocked at his door earlier than he forecasted. Death is as uncertain as life, its origins enveloped in circumstances beyond imagination, with consequences beyond control—betraying preconceptions and pushing one into the unknown.

In the last days of his life, Syed Mahmood is believed to have felt some premonition of death, as conveyed from a few instances reported by his close associates. About a month before his death, he got an aviary built in Sitapur near his cousin's residence. Mufti Syed Najmul Hasan Rizvi, a resident of Khairabad in Sitapur, reported[29] on the authority of his father that he saw tears rolling down the eyes of Syed Mahmood as he stood on the top of the aviary reciting a couplet,

'O resident of the palace high; verily ye shall be shortly buried in the earth.'

A contemporary of Syed Mahmood, Barrister Syed Ali Ausat, recalls that a week before his death, Mahmood while in his company recited a quatrain,[30] bearing the following translation:

*What is there if we are Strong; what is there*
*if we are Weak;*
*What is there if we are This, what is this*
*if we are That;*
*The High and the Low in this world is not material;*
*What is there if we are the Earth; what is there if we*
*are the Heavens.*
*The end was really near!*
(Translation by Barrister Syed Ali Ausat)

Probably this was his last-known foray into poetry.

Three days before his death, Mahmood is learnt to have persuaded Moulvi Ghulam Muhammad,[31] a divine of Sitapur, to stay with him. In his presence, Mahmood threw away all his wine bottles and repented before the Almighty for all his past sins.

In the first week of May in 1903, he caught fever and his condition deteriorated with each passing day. At around 11:00 AM on 8 May, while reading Surah Yusuf of the Holy Koran,[32] Mahmood breathed his last.

His body was brought to Aligarh by train from Sitapur via Lucknow. As the train reached the Aligarh railway station at 2:30 PM on 9 May, a huge crowd of people from all communities and professions had gathered to receive his body. Around 500 men are reported to have carried the coffin from there to Mahmood House, the residence of Musharraf Jahan Begum.

The chants of *Inna lillahi wa inna ilayhi raji'un*[33]—the funeral prayer for Muslims, meaning 'to Allah we belong, and to Him shall we return'—were recited as his body made its last journey and the soul its first one. He was laid to rest near his father's grave at the MAO College mosque, which presently houses the most august residential hall of AMU—the Sir Syed Hall.

*Mahmood Manzil, mausoleum of Syed Mahmood at AMU, where he was laid to rest*

Little did Mahmood realise that he had gained immortality in the short lifespan of 53 years. His contributions as a judge, author, intellectual and educationist illuminate the history of not just the Allahabad High Court and AMU but the entire nation.

# 6

# Shaping Interfaith Debate

National integration through tolerance is an ideal for all of us; it was a reality with Syed Mahmood.

His persona and depth of thoughts transcended the realm of materialistic life and found solace in mysticism. His knowledge of Arabic and Persian helped him develop deep insights in Sufism while his command over Sanskrit language made him an avid reader of Ramayana and attracted him towards the philosophy of Vedanta. Mahmood garnered heterogeneous experiences through his cross-cultural exposure—with his education commencing at a *maktab* and culminating at Cambridge via Queens College in the city of temples, pandits and ghats, Banaras.

As mentioned in Chapter 1, Mahmood moved to Banaras in 1868, where he was admitted to Queens' College, which was widely reputed at the time as a seminary of English language and literature. There, Mahmood had the benefit of the tutelage of distinguished Anglo-Sanskrit scholar and poet, Ralph T. Griffith—the famous translator of the Ramayana in English and author of the book of poems titled *Idylls from the Sanskrit*. Queens' College was envisioned as an alchemy of the Banaras Sanskrit College and the English Seminary. It adhered to a unique integrated pattern of education conscientiously assimilating the knowledge of the East and the West. Coincidentally, its educational philosophy and ideals mirrored those of Sir Syed Ahmad Khan, and are believed to have largely shaped Syed Mahmood's understanding of educational philosophy and pedagogy.

Moreover, being a son to a social reformer, author and civil servant added to his understanding of religion and cultures. His closest known friends were A.M. Bose (whom Mahmood fondly referred to as 'my tutor' when he was at Cambridge), Satish Chandra Banerji, Tej Bahadur Sapru and George E.A. Ross. Satish Chandra Banerji, in one of his articles in *Hindustan Review*, wrote that Mahmood was a true liberal and a friend of progress; he visualised perfect fellowship between Hindus and Muslims and wanted them to join hands as one kin. The article stated:

> Mr Mahmood was a man of liberal sympathies and a true friend of progress. He had the highest regard for Mr A.M. Bose (he would fondly refer to him as 'my tutor when I was an undergraduate at Cambridge') and his friends among Hindus were, I believe, quite as numerous as among the Mohamdans. He certainly did not view the Indian National Congress as 'dread' as some of his co-religionist who contribute Aligarh Institute Gazette, profess to; and I have reason to believe that if Mr Surendra Nath Banerjee and Mr A.M. Bose had approached him properly, he might have presided over the annual deliberations of the national body. He once told me at Lucknow that he was seriously thinking about this matter, that he had sympathy

> with the movement, and that he was prepared to accept many of the resolutions adopted at meetings of the Indian National Congress. Unfortunately not having studied the science of politics with any thoroughness I do not care to dabble in politics, and so I did not push the matter further. But that Mr Mahmood was [a] much more clear sighted man and had the *true cause of his mother country more deeply at heart than any self styled politicians,* both Hindus and Mussalman, who rush to print or clamber up the platform, I have not the least doubt, Mr Mahmood was [a] proud man, he was a hot tempered man, he had his fixed ideas (who has not?) but he had no patience with hypocrisy, with pettiness, with servility and knee-truckling. I heard from my father 18 years ago that Mr Mahmood used to deplore the absence of a national leader in India and expressed hope that Bengal might one day give to the country such a leader. True it is that distance lends disenchantment to this view. There can be no doubt however, that he would have liked to see perfect fellowship among Hindus and Mussalmans, and he would often say to me 'you are a Brahman among Hindus, I am a Syed among Mussalmans; let us join hands together as of one kin.'[1] [emphasis added]

Interestingly, according to Lieutenant Colonel G.F.I. Graham, the dinner hosted in honour of Mahmood's return from London as barrister was the first dinner in the NWP at which Muslims, Hindus and English gentlemen sat down together.[2]

At the aforementioned occasion, Mahmood delivered a short speech epitomising the composite culture and oneness of India in fostering unity amongst the countrymen. He said:

> Having differences in religion does not eradicate the entire influence of those matters in which Muslims and Hindus work together. Those who know me well, also know that my training and upbringing was done in such a manner and in such an atmosphere that I value national unity (*hum watani*) and its enthusiasm and ideas above all other ideas of humanity. Differences in religion are not something by which the brotherly relationship engendered by national unity is done away. . ..[3]

Mahmood's decision to appoint Theodore Beck as first the principal and later the honorary treasurer of MAO College was rooted in his conviction of merit over religion or region. Furthermore, in the scheme for the proposed MAO College presented before the fund committee on 10 February 1873, he recommended Sanskrit to be taught as an optional language.[4] The scheme provided the following:

> The course of study at the lower department of the College will comprise the following subjects.
>
> Any two of the following languages:
>
> - Arabic (language and literature)
> - English (language and literature)
> - Sanskrit (language and literature)
> - Latin (language and literature)
> - Greek (language and literature)

Similarly, the course of study of the upper department of the college included a compulsory subject on ancient Indian languages, available with the following combinations:

1. Sanskrit with Zend, Persian and philology
2. Sanskrit with Prakriti and Pali and philology[5]

Other combinations available were:

1. Arabic with Hebrew and Syriac and comparative philology of the Semitic language
2. English with Anglo-Saxon and comparative philology of the Teutonic stock of languages
3. Greek and Latin with philology

He steered the policy of non-interference in religious beliefs and practices of the non-Muslim students and strived for harmonious coexistence in the residential life at the college. As evident from the MAO College scheme prepared by him, he framed a secular and modern curriculum for MAO College with a balance of religious and scientific education. The scheme expressly stated, 'Of course every student will have a perfect right to study the theology of his religion in particular.'[6]

In another instance, when Principal Theodore Beck removed the teacher of Sanskrit from service and discontinued Sanskrit instructions, Mahmood got him reinstated.

A multilinguist himself, he did not harbour a bias in favour of or against English. In fact, he placed equal emphasis on instructions in oriental languages and got interlanguage texts translated for proper dissemination of knowledge. At a conference in Allahabad, Mahmood urged his audience to undertake research on ancient Indian languages, trace the contribution of Muslims in the development of such languages and determine their proficiency in such languages.[7]

Mahmood dressed every diversity in his strong sense of honour that was embedded in the moral and civilisational philosophy of Bharat. These moorings prompted him to write a book on the impact of Hindu culture on Muslims in India, which unfortunately, he could not complete as time stood still for him at a relatively early age. The motivation for undertaking such work arose from him wanting to dispel the misunderstanding that Muslims do not take enough interest in the scriptures and texts of Hindu religion and culture. Even today, efforts to highlight writings of such work done by Muslims does not commensurate with the importance of the need to accentuate such works.

Freedom of religion and faith equality was an article of faith for Mahmood. In his *Calcutta Review* article 'British Rule in India: Does It owe Origin to Conquest, and Its Maintenance to Physical Force' (1879)—directed at an audience of British officials and widely circulated in the higher echelons in Britain—he waxed eloquent to the Raj to earnestly adhere to the values of tolerance, humanity and mutual respect as the governance core for their stable rule in India. Illustrating the reign of Aurangzeb, whose wanton disregard for these values was the cause of downfall of Mughal rule, Mahmood wrote:

> The reign of Aurangzeb, with all its martial glory and powerful administration, with all its conquests

> and physical force, succumbed to the law of nature, succumbed to the ardent and originally defensive opposition of the pious Brahmin, to the curses of the suffering devotee, to the united force of exasperated millions. He died whilst still at the head of a great campaign: the most glorious and the most inglorious of India's Mohammedan rulers, the degrader of his ancestral heritage, the degrader of race and religion. He lies beneath the dust of those very plains which had seen his greatest martial achievements and had felt his greatest force.[8]

In Mahmood's estimation, Aurangzeb was a bad politician—his statesmanship relied for its success on martial discipline and physical force. He failed to appreciate the potential of 'amicable modes' and 'power of moral causes' that were relied upon by his ancestors, especially Akbar, in administration. He wrote:

> What was it that made the reign of Akbar so illustrious and prosperous . . . . whose armies were far lesser than he (Aurangzeb) mustered
>
> . . .
>
> The power of moral causes he entirely ignored; the feelings of his subjects he did not consult. He learnt the noble lesson but too late, that it is,
>
> '—*more humane, more heavenly; first*
> *By winning words to conquer willing hearts*
> *And make persuasion do the work of fear.*'[9]

Mahmood reproaches Aurangzeb for not paying heed to the advice of Maharaja Jaswant Singh of Jodhpur against his oppressive policies, an advice Mahmood deemed as 'unsurpassed in its originality of wisdom, its earnestness of solicitude, its beauty of taste, and above all, its soundness of policy'. Relevant extracts of Maharaja's letter to Aurangzeb were reproduced by Mahmood in his article. The Maharaja wrote:

> During your Majesty's reign, many have been alienated from the empire and further losses must ensue, since the devastation and the rapine reign without restraint . . . How can the dignity of a sovereign be preserved who employs his power in extracting heavy tributes from a people miserably reduced? At this juncture, it is said, from East to West, that the Emperor of Hindustan, jealous of the poor Hindu devotee, will exact tribute from Brahmans, *et cetera*; that regardless of the honour of his Timurian ancestry, he condescends to exercise his strength against the inoffensive religious recluse.
>
> . . . If your Majesty places any faith in those books by distinction called divine, you may there learn that God is the God of all mankind, not of Mussalmans only. The *Pagan* and the *Moslem* stand alike before him. . . In your mosques, it is in His name that the call to prayer is uttered. In the house of idols, where bells are rung, it is still He that is the object of adoration. *To vilify the religious customs of other men is to set at naught the will of the Almighty. When we deface a picture, we necessarily incur the resentment of the painter.*[10] [emphasis added]

Mahmood also referred to the distinction drawn by the Maharaja in the state of affairs during the reigns of Aurangzeb's predecessors. It read:

> Your royal ancestor, M. Jalaludin Akbar, conducted the affairs of the empire in dignity and safety for fifty-two years, keeping every tribe and class in peace and prosperity; whether they were followers of Jesus, or of Moses, or Muhammad; were they Brahmans, were they (atheists); or equally enjoyed his countenance and favour, in so much that his subjects distinguished him by the title of 'Protector of the Human Race.'
>
> . . .
>
> Jahangir also extended for a period of twenty-two years the shadow of his protection over his people's heads; successful by constant fidelity to his allies, and vigorous exertions in the affairs of State.
>
> . . .
>
> Nor less did the illustrious Shah Jahan, by a propitious reign of thirty-two years, acquire to himself immortal fame, the just reward of clemency and righteousness.[11]

With Mahmood's vociferous denunciation of Aurangzeb's intolerance, it comes as no surprise that he rather admired the enlightened philosophy of Dara Shikoh—the eldest Mughal prince murdered by Aurangzeb in a battle for the throne—widely believed to be the founder of academic movement of interfaith understanding in India. Dara Shikoh advocated that cordial relationships between people of different faiths can be developed by finding commonality in their religious scriptures. His famous work, *Majma al-Bahrain* or confluence of two oceans, which explored similarities between Hinduism and Islam, was referred by Mahmood for his two books on Muslim law—*Kitab al-Talaq* and *Kitab al-Shuf'ah*. In the 100th year of its establishment, AMU established the 'Dara Shikoh Centre for Interfaith Dialogue and Understanding' to carry forward the legacy of its founders in promoting national integration through peaceful coexistence.[12]

In 1893, a public bismillah ceremony was organised for Mahmood's son, Syed Ross Masood. Interestingly, he honoured the wish of his dear friend George E.A. Ross by naming his only child Ross Masood after him. The child Ross had an eclectic introduction to life—in his bismillah ceremony, he sat in the lap of Raja Jai Kishan Das, a confidant of his grandfather Sir Syed. Generally, as a matter of tradition, the child is made to sit in the lap of the eldest member of the family.

*Bismillah ceremony of Syed Mahmood's son, Ross Masood*

In the foregoing pages of this book, Syed Mahmood's instrumental role in the educational movement of 19th-century India has been described. His conviction in the ideals of the movement was stimulated from a distressing realisation—Indian minds were obscured by dogmas that betrayed scientific outlook and rationality. While it is true that the cause of 'Muslim education' had captured Mahmood's special attention, it was not a digression from the overarching objective of the movement—all Indians, irrespective of faith, should come together against the scourge of illiteracy. The reason for Mahmood's focus on Muslim education is based on his findings that Hindus had already ventured towards modern education much before Muslims. The tussle between conservatives and reformists had been settled much earlier among them than the Muslims. We have alluded to this in the previous chapter, in the discussion on Mahmood's book *A History of English Education in India*.

As a liberal embodying scientific temperament, rationality and cosmopolitanism, Mahmood could not allow his altruism to be impeded by the narrow and parochial considerations of faith. In his speech at the foundation stone–laying ceremony of MAO College, he specifically addressed the Hindu brethren and expressed gratitude for their contributions to the college. He said:

> To our Hindu friends also our thanks are largely due. Foremost among them is the name remembered by us no less sorrow than gratitude, of His Highness Sri Maharao Rajah Mohandar Singh, Mohandar Bahadoor, G.C.S.I., and the late Maharaja of

Patiala whose munificent contributions to the college amount to no less than ₹ 58,000 [sic]. Their Highness the Maharaja of Vizianagram, K.C.S.I., and the Maharaja of Banaras [sic] head the list which includes the names of many liberal minded Hindu gentlemen whose philanthropy forbids them to recognise distinctions of race and creed. In their large-hearted public spirit we see the germs of that true toleration and genuine sympathy which is the direct result of peace and good government.

The Mohammedan Anglo Oriental Fund Committee is determined to invite subscriptions from the English community as well as members of their own faith. Nor did the Committee omit to ask the aid of Hindu fellow-countrymen; for they felt that neither race nor creed would, with rightly thinking men, stand in their way of support to an undertaking such as theirs. Their expectations have in both cases been amply justified, and it is our pleasant duty to make mention of the chief benefactors of this college. . .

*The establishment of the College is based upon principles of toleration and progress and such as find no parallel in the annals of the East.*[13] [emphasis added]

Later in his speech he read out a ghazal from *Shams-i Tabriz*, the influential Persian philosopher and teacher of Jalal al-Dīn Rūmī:

*What shall I do, O ye Muslims, for I do not know myself anymore;*
*I am neither Christian, nor Jew, nor Zoroastrian, nor Muslim.*

In reference to the aforementioned ghazal, he explained that the lines contained in it did not mean that the Sufi saint mentioned in it had ceased to be a Muslim. It rather meant that his utterance was in compassion for all, irrespective of their religion.

As the first Muslim high court judge, Mahmood never questioned the legitimacy of non-Muslims deciding matters pertaining to Islamic law. In fact, he himself extensively relied on ancient Hindu texts in several of his decisions governing Hindu law. One would have assumed that he would not be so exhaustive on the subject of Hindu law. However, in several cases on that subject too, he displayed the same depth of knowledge of the original texts. He observed: 'To import foreign ideas and bring them to bear upon interpreting Sanskrit texts when modes of interpretation sanctioned by Hindu logicians of the highest authority are forthcoming is an obvious error.'[14]

In Chapter 4, we have explained in detail the seminal contribution of Justice Mahmood to the development of Hindu law jurisprudence based on his interpretation of original ancient Hindu texts such as Sancha, Lichita, Manu, Harita, Shastras, Mayukha, Yajnavalkya, Vijneshwara, Nandapandita and the texts of Nandapandita. Of these, he widely quoted Manu, the first great dharma-shastric text, saying that it was the sacred duty of the king to 'enquire into the laws of castes, districts, guilds, and families, and settle (or protect) the peculiar law of each'.

Amongst his most reformative judicial contributions, synthesising Hindu and Muslim laws with common law is a marker. Words of Justice Sunil Ambwani, former chief justice of Rajasthan High Court and judge at the Allahabad High Court, will suffice:

> Of all the judges, who had taken part in the deliberations of the Allahabad High Court since its establishment, Mr Justice Syed Mahmood played an important part in development of law. His short tenure of six years brought about synthesis between ancient Hindu and Mohammedan laws and the common law imbued directly or through statutes from England. He was perhaps the first and remains unexcelled [sic]. His distant footsteps still echo through the corridors of time . . .
>
> In the rule of personal laws of Hindus and Mohammedan his expositions are texts. He travelled into regions left unexplored by the commentators on the text and his judgments like sun light poring through the clouds revealed many a hidden truth.[15]

Mahmood was a man of faith and interfaith, with a commitment to the pillars on which independent India was founded—judicial freedom (judicial), empowerment (education) and tolerance (religious).

## Appendix I

# Timeline of the Life of Syed Mahmood

1850: Born in Delhi to Sir Syed Ahmad Khan and Parsa Begum

1854: Bi'smillah Ceremony held and started taking lessons of Koran

1857: The first battle of Independence—resulting in a gap in his formal education

1858: Migrated to Moradabad with Sir Syed, who was transferred to Moradabad as *sadr amin*. Mahmood was enrolled at a Persian school there.

1862: Mother (Parsa Begum) died in Moradabad

1862: Migrated to Ghazipur with his father and commenced taking lessons in English from a Bengali tutor

1864: Moved to Aligarh with Sir Syed

1864: Enrolled at the Government Vernacular School of Aligarh

1864: Delivered his first speech at the Scientific Society

1866: Delivered his second speech at the Scientific Society

1868: Enrolled as a student at Queens, College, Banaras

1869: Stood first in the order of merit in his high school examination at Queens, College, Banaras

1869: Secured a government scholarship and moved to England

1869: Admitted to Lincoln's Inn

1870: Admitted to Christ's College, Cambridge University

1871: Won the English Prize at Christ's College

1872: Qualified as a Barrister/Bar-at-law

1872: Prepared the first scheme for MAO College in Urdu titled '*Yuniwirsity Kaimbirij*'

1872: Returned to India

1873: Began law practice before the NWP High Court. Also drafted the revised scheme for MAO College, which was presented before the MAO College Fund Committee

1876: Wrote a commentary on the Indian Evidence Act, 1872

1877: Delivered the inaugural address at the foundation stone – laying ceremony of MAO College

1879: Joined the Indian Civil Service as district judge

1881: Attached to the state of Hyderabad, on deputation

1882: First officiating appointment as a judge of the Allahabad High Court

1882: Appointed as a member of the Indian Education Commission (Hunter Commission)

1883: Visited England to recruit a headmaster for MAO College from Cambridge University

1884: Second officiating appointment as a judge of the Allahabad High Court

1886: Third officiating appointment as a judge of the Allahabad High Court

1887: Fourth officiating appointment as a judge of the Allahabad High Court. Also elevated as a permanent judge of the Allahabad High Court

1888: Married Musharraf Jahan Begum

1889: Blessed by the birth of his son, Ross Masood

1893: Resigned from judgeship of the high court and restarted law practice

1893: Delivered the first of his series of lectures at the All India Muhammadan Educational Conference

1894: Nominated to the legislative council of NWP and Oudh

1894: Death of his brother, Syed Hamid

1895: Authored the book *A History of English Education in India*

1898: Death of his father, Sir Syed Ahmad Khan, at Aligarh

1898: Assumed the office of secretary, MAO College

1899: Resigned as secretary, MAO College and assumed the office of president, MAO College

1901: Removed as president, MAO College and subsequently nominated as a visitor of MAO College

1901: Moved to Sitapur to stay with his cousin, Syed Muhammad Ahmad

1903: Death

# Appendix II

# Genealogy of Syed Mahmood

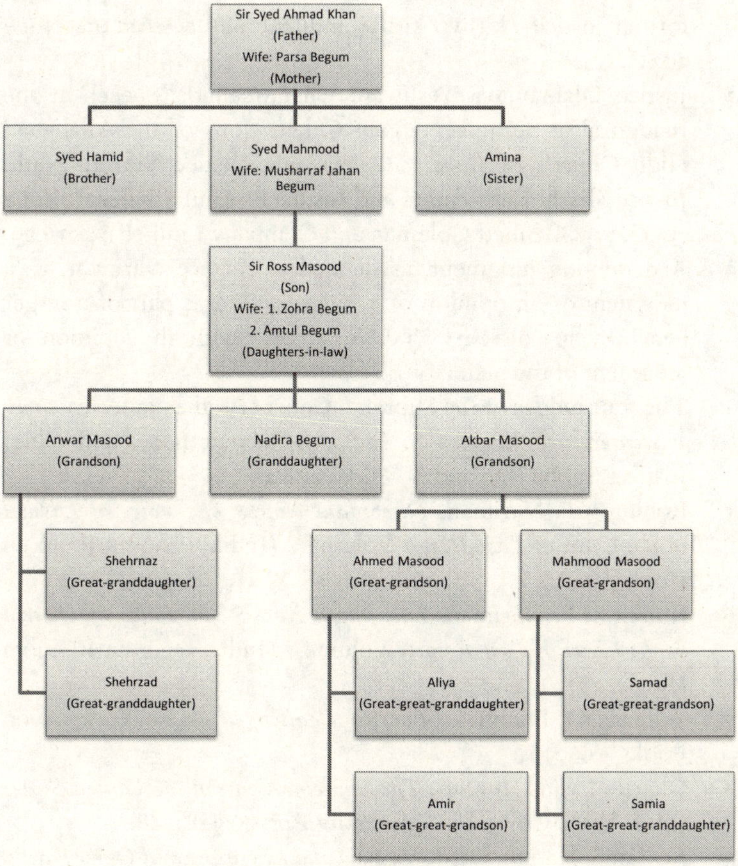

# NOTES

## INTRODUCTION

1 Justice Michael Kirby, 5th Bar Association of India Lecture, Hilton Hotel, New Delhi, 6 January 1997. Available at: https://www.hcourt.gov.au/assets/publications/speeches/former-justices/kirbyj/kirbyj_indialt.htm (accessed on 1 June 2021).

2 Justice Dhananjaya Yeshwant Chandrachud. 'Speech at the Inaugural at Sesquicentennial Celebrations of the Allahabad High Court'. In *Gavel and Pen*, eds. Justice Vikram Nath, Justice Shashi Kant Gupta and Justice B. Amit Sthalekar, Vol 2 (Lucknow: Bennett Coleman and Company Limited), 2016 79.

3 A dissenting judgment, as defined by Justice Nariman, is 'a judgment or an opinion of a judge, sitting as part of a larger bench, who 'dissents' (i.e. disagrees) with the opinion or judgment of the majority.

4 The four judges of the Supreme Court of India named as *Great Dissenters* are Justices S. Fazl Ali, Vivian Bose, and Chief Justices Subba Rao and M. Hidayatullah.

5 Rohinton F. Nariman, *Discordant Notes: The Voice of Dissent in the Court of Last Resort* Volume 2 (India: Penguin Random House, 2021), 4.

6 Rohinton F. Nariman, *Discordant Notes: The Voice of Dissent in the Court of Last Resort,* Volume 1 (India: Penguin Random House, 2021), 41.

7 William O. Douglas, *America Challenged* (New York: Avon Books, 1960), 4.

8 Charles Evans Hughes, *The Supreme Court of the United States* (New York: Columbia University Press, 1928), 28.

9 Benjamin Nathan Cardozo, *Law and Literature and Other Essays and Addresses* (New York: Harcourt, Brace & Co. 1931), 36.

10 William O. Douglas, 'The Dissent: A Safeguard of Democracy', *Journal of American Judicature Society*, 32, no. 4 (December 1948): 106–107.

11 All India Reporter 2020 Supreme Court 5026.
12 (1885) Indian Law Reports 7 Allahabad 775.
13 (2017) 9 Supreme Court Cases 1.
14 Para 420 of *Shayara Bano v. Union of India*, Manupatra Online Legal Database/Supreme Court/1031/2017.
15 (1891) Indian Law Reports 13 Allahabad 171.
16 (1884) Indian Law Reports 6 Allahabad 509.
17 *Centenary High Court of Judicature at Allahabad Commemoration 1866–1966 Volume*. Allahabad: Allahabad High Court Centenary Commemoration Volume Committee, Volume II. Available at: http://www.allahabadhighcourt.in/event/Justice_Syed_Mahmood_M_Hidayatullah.pdf (accessed on 10 June 2021)
18 Brojendra Mitter, *Indian Judges: Biographical and Critical Sketches with Portraits* (Madras: GA Natesan and Company, 1932).
19 An informal association of English artists and intellectuals, such as, Lytton Strachey, John Keynes and E.M. Forster, in the first half of the 20th century. Largely drawn from the University of Cambridge and King's College, they studied together near Bloomsbury, London.
20 Scheherazade Tilat Alim. 'This was a Man', *Aligarh Law Journal* 5, (1973): 397.
21 (1885) Indian Law Reports 7 Allahabad 822.

## CHAPTER 1 THE JOURNEY BEGINS: CHILDHOOD, EDUCATION AND FAMILY

1 Al Koran: Chapter 17 Verse 79.
2 North-western province was an administrative region in British India from 1836 to 1902 consisting of present-day Uttar Pradesh (UP) excluding the region of Oudh.
3 Khwaja Altaf Husain Hali, *Hayat-i-Jawed*, trans. Rafi Ahmed Alavi (Aligarh: Sir Syed Academy, Aligarh Muslim University, 2008) 57–58.
4 The *bismillah* ceremony marks the beginning of the religious education of a Muslim child. Preferably held at the age of four years, four months, four days, the child is made to recite the opening words of the Koran.
5 *Maktab* refers to a school attached to a mosque.

6 Alan Guenther, 'Syed Mahmood and the Transformation of Muslim Law in India' (Unpublished PhD thesis, Institute of Islamic Studies, McGill University, Canada, 2004) 39.

7 Ibid.

8 David Lelyveld, 'Macaulay's Curse: Sir Syed and Syed Mahmood'. In *Sir Syed Ahmad Khan: A Centenary Tribute*, ed. Asloob Ahmad Ansari (Delhi: Adam Publishers, 2001), 196.

9 *Tabeen-ul-Kalam* is a commentary on the Holy Bible written by Sir Syed Ahmad Khan published in three volumes. The first part dealt with the Bible as a whole, the second with the *Genesis* and the third with the *Gospels of Saint Matthew*. In a lecture delivered in 1883, Sir Syed informed the audience that the first volume of *Tabeen-ul-Kalam* published and was available for sale.

10 Alan Guenther, 'Syed Mahmood and the Transformation of Muslim Law in India' (Unpublished PhD thesis: Institute of Islamic Studies, McGill University, Canada, 2004), 40.

11 Ibid.

12 The Scientific Society was established at Gazipur in December 1862 by Sir Syed Ahmad Khan to serve two primary objectives: firstly, to discover and publish all rare oriental manuscripts on non-religious subject matter; and secondly, to translate the available European literature on arts and science in languages commonly known to the people of northern India.

13 *Aligarh Institute Gazette*. Aligarh, 30 March 1866.

14 Maulana Ahsan Marehrvi, *Aligarh Magazine* (Aligarh: Jamia Barqi Press, 1938), 93.

15 Prof. Azarmi Dukht Safavi is an internationally acclaimed Persian scholar and presently the Tagore National Fellow for Cultural Research (TNFCR) by the Ministry of Culture, Government of India.

16 David Lelyveld, 'Macaulay's Curse: Sir Syed and Syed Mahmood'. In *Sir Syed Ahmad Khan: A Centenary Tribute*, ed. Asloob Ahmad Ansari (Delhi: Adam Publishers, 2001), 198.

17 'Michaelmas' term is the first term of the academic year in a number of English-speaking universities and schools in the northern hemisphere, especially in the United Kingdom. Michaelmas term derives its name from the feast of St Michael and All Angels, which falls on 29 September.

18 Anand Mohan Bose was a supporter of the Brahmo Samaj and a contemporary of Syed Mahmood at Christ's College, Cambridge. He practised law in British India, co-founded the Indian National Association and later became a senior leader of the Indian National Congress.

19 *The Fleur-de-Lys*. Christ's College, 17 December 1870, 10–11.

20 The Royal Asiatic Society of Great Britain and Ireland was founded by the eminent Sanskrit scholar Henry Thomas Colebrooke on 15 March 1823. It received its Royal Charter from King George IV on 11 August 1824 'for the investigation of subjects connected with and for the encouragement of science, literature and the arts in relation to Asia'. The society provides a forum for those who are interested in the history, languages, cultures and religions of Asia to meet and exchange ideas. It also conducts lectures and seminars on a regular basis.

21 Gur Dayal Srivastava, 'Mr Justice Mahmood', 1966. Available at http://www.allahabadhighcourt.in/event/MrJusticeMahmoodGDSrivastava.html (accessed on 7 February 2021).

22 Syed Mahmood, 'Syed Mahmood's letter dated 8 September 1893 addressed to Hon'ble J.D. La Touche, Chief Secretary to the Government of NWP and Oudh'. In *Justice Syed Mahmood Papers*, ed. Iqbal Husain (Aligarh Muslim University, Aligarh: Sir Syed Academy, 2005), 63.

23 David Lelyveld, *Aligarh's First Generation: Muslim Solidarity in British India* (Princeton, New Jersey: Princeton University Press, 1978), 3.

24 George Farquhar Irving Graham, *The Life and Work of Sir Syed Ahmed Khan* (Delhi: Idarah-i-Adabiyat-i-Delli, 1974), 282.

25 Syed Mahmood, 'British Rule in India: Does it Owe its Origin to Conquest, and Its Maintenance to Physical Force?', *Calcutta Review* 68, (1879): 2.

26 Ibid. 8.

27 Ibid. 1–2.

28 David Lelyveld speculates that the most plausible reason as his father's insistence that he return to India.

29 Syed Mahmood was admitted to Lincoln's Inn on 10 May 1869 and got himself enrolled as a barrister in the High Court of Judicature at Allahabad in 1872.

On 16 December 1872, *The Pioneer*, a newspaper daily, reported that the High Court of the NWP, on the motion of the government advocate, had enrolled Syed Mahmood, Esquire, of Christ's College, Cambridge and Lincoln's Inn, Barrister-at-Law, as an advocate of the court.

30 George Farquhar Irving Graham, *The Life and Work of Sir Syed Ahmed Khan* (Delhi: Idarah-i-Adabiyat-i-Delli, 1974), 250–251.

31 Shamsur Rahman Faruqi, *From Antiquary to Social Revolutionary: Syed Ahmad Khan and the Colonial Experience* (AMU, Aligarh: Sir Syed Academy, 2007), 4.

32 Syed Mahmood, 'Dosti' in *Tahzib ul-Akhlaq* (Aligarh: Aligarh Scientific Society, 1871), 2:3–4.

33 Syed Mahmood, 'Shiddat-i-Itqa' in *Tahzib ul-Akhlaq*, (Aligarh: Aligarh Scientific Society, 1871), 2:78–80.

34 Sir Tej Bahadur Sapru was a contemporary and close friend of Barrister Mahmood at the Allahabad High Court Bar. He later rose to eminence as a jurist and statesman.

35 *Pandit* is a learned Brahmin scholar who makes learning in Sanskrit, Hindu philosophy and religion his primary duty and teaches it.

36 *Aligarh Institute Gazette*, 27 June 1903.

37 Ibid.

38 Ibid.

39 Ibid.

40 Ibid.

41 Ibid.

42 Mohammad Ameen Zuberi, *Tazkira-e-Syed Mahmood* (Aligarh: Institute Press, year not known), 48–49.

43 *Aligarh Institute Gazette*, Aligarh, 18 June 1924.

44 Mohammad Ameen Zuberi, *Tazkira-e-Syed Mahmood* (Aligarh: Institute Press, year not known), 47.

45 Ibid. 49.

46 David Lelyveld, 'Macaulay's Curse: Sir Syed and Syed Mahmood' In *Sir Syed Ahmad Khan: A Centenary Tribute*, ed. Asloob Ahmad Ansari (Delhi: Adam Publishers, 2001), 203.

47 Khwaja Altaf Husain Hali, *Hayat-i-Jawed: A Biographical Account of Sir Syed Ahmad Khan*, trans. Rafi Ahmad Alavi (Aligarh Muslim University: Aligarh, 2008) 119.

48 'Sir Syed House', 2021. Available at: https://www.amu.ac.in/academies/sir-syed-academy/home-page (accessed on 5 February 2021).
49 Faiza Abbasi, *Women in AMU at 100* (Aligarh: Publications Division, Aligarh Muslim University), 13.
50 Ibid.
51 'Begum Azeezun Nisa Hall', 2021. Available at: https://www.amu.ac.in/halls/begum-azzezun-nisa-hall. (accessed on 12 March 2021).
52 Jalil Ahmad Kidwai, *A Forgotten Hero of Our Struggle*, (Karachi: Ross Masood Education and Culture Society of Pakistan, 1985).
53 E. A. Molony in his letter dated 10 August 1889 addressed to J. O. Miller, Secretary to the Lt. Governor of NWP and Oudh, mentioned the letters he received from Musharraf Jahan Begum, wife of Justice Syed Mahmood.
54 Faiza Abbasi, *Women in AMU at 100* (Aligarh: Publications Division, Aligarh Muslim University), 14.
55 Further discussion on Theodore Morison is made in Chapter 2.
56 *Aligarh Institute Gazette*, 28 September 1910.
57 Ibid.
58 Shyam Krishna Bhatnagar, *History of the M.A.O. College* (AMU, Aligarh: Sir Syed Hall Publication, 1969), 309.
59 *Anjuman Taraqi-Urdu* was founded in 1903. It is an all-India body with a wide network of over 600 branches across India working for the promotion of Urdu language. In 2011, the organisation had published the biography of Sir Ross Masood.

## CHAPTER 2 EDUCATIONIST: CONTRIBUTION TO THE ALIGARH MUSLIM UNIVERSITY

1 Hamilton Alexander Rosskeen Gibb, *Mohammedanism* (New York: Oxford University Press, 1996), 181.
2 Sheikh Mumtaz Husain Jaunpuri, 'Sir Syed Ahmad Aur Zindagi Ka Naya Shaoor', *Aligarh Magazine–Special Aligarh Number*, (1953).
3 Shan Muhammad, *The Aligarh Movement: A Concise Study*, (Aligarh: Educational Book House, 1999), 98–99.
4 Anis Ansari, 'Syed Mahmood: His Life and Works', *Aligarh Law Journal* 5 (1973):11.

5 The Hunter Commission is officially the Indian Education Commission. Mahmood's contribution to the commission is discussed in Chapter 5.

6 *Aligarh Institute Gazette*, Aligarh, 5 August 1992.

7 The Aligarh Movement started in the aftermath of the Revolt of 1857. It aimed to extricate the Muslim society from obscurantism and inculcate in them the liberal and Western education along with the true teachings of Islam. It is categorised as one of the most influential and pervading movement touching all spheres of Muslim activities—social, educational, religious and cultural.

8 Shyam Krishna Bhatnagar, *History of the MAO College of Aligarh* (AMU, Aligarh: Sir Syed Hall Publication, 1969), 15.

9 Iqbal Hussain, *Justice Syed Mahmood Papers* (AMU, Aligarh: Sir Syed Academy, 2005), vii.

10 Shafey Kidwai, 'Female Education'. In *Sir Syed Ahmad Khan: Reason, Religion and Nation* (India: Routledge, 2021), 153.

11 David Lelyveld, 'Macaulay's Curse: Sir Syed and Syed Mahmood'. In *Sir Syed Ahmad Khan: A Centenary Tribute*, ed. Asloob Ahmad Ansari (Delhi: Adam Publishers, 2001), 194–195.

12 Shan Muhammad, *The Aligarh Movement: A Concise Study* (Aligarh: Educational Book House, 1999), 97.

13 Shyam Krishna Bhatnagar, *History of the MAO College of Aligarh* (AMU, Aligarh: Sir Syed Hall Publication, 1969), 34.

14 David Lelyveld, 'Macaulay's Curse: Sir Syed and Syed Mahmood'. In *Sir Syed Ahmad Khan: A Centenary Tribute*, ed. Asloob Ahmad Ansari (Delhi: Adam Publishers, 2001), 200.

15 *Aligarh Institute Gazette*. Aligarh, 22 March 1872.

16 An important ingredient of this plan was an essay that Syed Mahmud sent in from Cambridge in February; he proposed the establishment of a residential college 'where Muslims alone would be able to obtain an education according to their wishes'.

17 David Lelyveld, *Aligarh's First Generation: Muslim Solidarity in British India* (Princeton, New Jersey: Princeton University Press, 1978), 138.

18 Ibid.

19 Ibid.

20 Syed Mahmood, 'A Scheme for the Proposed Mohammedan Anglo Oriental College'. In *Justice Syed Mahmood Papers*, ed. Iqbal Husain (Aligarh Muslim University, Aligarh: Sir Syed Academy, 2005), 220.

21 Ibid. 221.

22 Ibid. 221.

23 Ibid. 224.

24 Ibid. 223–224.

25 Ibid. 224.

26 Moulvi Samiullah Khan was a close associate of Sir Syed. Syed Mahmood started his law practice as a junior to Moulvi Samiullah.

27 Syed Mahmood, 'Syed Mahmood's Letter Dated 27 November 1898 Addressed to Theodore Beck, Principal and Registrar MAO College'. In *Justice Syed Mahmood Papers*, ed. Iqbal Husain (Aligarh Muslim University, Aligarh: Sir Syed Academy, 2005), 356.

28 Ibid. 357.

29 Ibid. 358.

30 Mohammad Nasir, 'A Symbol of India's Composite Culture'. Available at: https://openthemagazine.com/columns/symbol-indias-composite-culture/ (accessed on 12 February 2021)

31 'Speech Delivered by Hon'ble Prime Minister Shri Narendra Modi at the Centenary Celebrations Programme dated 22 December 2020', *The Aligarh Institute Gazette-Centenary Special Issue* (AMU, Aligarh: Sir Syed Academy, 2020), 1–12. *Available at: https://digital.amu.ac.in/gazette/#page/2* (accessed on 21 July 2021).

32 Ministry of Human Resource Development, *National Education Policy 2020* (New Delhi: Government of India), 33.

33 Ibid.

34 Ibid. 45.

35 Ibid. 47.

36 Shyam Krishna Bhatnagar, *History of the M.A.O. College* (Aligarh: Sir Syed Hall Publication, 1969), 103.

37 Theodore Morrison, *The History of the M.A.O. College, Aligarh: From its Foundation to the Year 1903: Together with the Annual Report for the Year 1902-1903 and Appendices* (Allahabad: Pioneer Press, 1903), 44–45.

38 Syed Mahmood, 'Syed Mahmood's Letter Dated 8 September 1893 Addressed to Hon'ble J.D. La Touche, Chief Secretary to the Government of NWP and Oudh'. In *Justice Syed Mahmood Papers*, ed. Iqbal Husain (Aligarh Muslim University, Aligarh: Sir Syed Academy, 2005), 59–60.

39 Shyam Krishna Bhatnagar, *History of the M.A.O. College* (Aligarh: Sir Syed Hall Publication, 1969), 127.

40 Mohammad Nasir, 'Realising the Idea of a University: Faculties and Departments-Faculty of Law'. In *A History of Aligarh Muslim University 1920–2020*, ed. M.A. Siddiqui, R. Abrar, F. Abbasi (Lucknow: Bennett Coleman and Company, Times of India Group, 2021), 78–79.

41 *Aligarh Institute Gazette*. Aligarh, 18 March 1890.

42 *Aligarh Institute Gazette*. Aligarh, 10 September 1890.

43 *Munsif*–An Arabic term meaning equitable or just: a decider of what is just, an arbitrator, a judge; applied under the British government to a native civil judge of first or lowest rank.

44 *Sadr Amin*–An Arabic term meaning chief commissioner or arbitrator, the title of a class of native civil judges under the British government.

45 *Sadr or Sadr-us-Sudoor*–An Arabic term referring to the chief judge, the chancellor; under the Muhammadan government, he was especially charged with the investigation of the cases of all those who applied to the sovereign for grants of revenue; he had also the charge of *wakf* property or religious endowments, and the appointment of *kazis* and other law officers.

46 Shafey Kidwai, *Sir Syed Ahmad Khan: Reason, Religion and Nation* (India: Routledge, 2021), 67.

47 *Kazi*–An Arabic term used to refer to a Muhammadan judge; an officer appointed by the government to administer both civil and criminal law, chiefly in towns, according to the principles of the Koran. The institution of *kaz*is had been granted legal sanction during the Mughal rule. However, under the British administration, their judicial functions were repealed, except for general superintendence and legalisation of religious ceremonies of marriage, funerals and other domestic occurrences amongst the Muslims.

48 Shafey Kidwai, *Sir Syed Ahmad Khan: Reason Religion and Nation* (India: Routledge, 2021).

49 'Recollections of a Student', *Aligarh Institute Gazette*, Aligarh, 20 June 1903.

50 'Recollections of a Student', *Aligarh Institute Gazette*, Aligarh, 27 June 1903.

51 Ibid.

52 John Austin (1790–1859) was a British attorney and educator who became well known for his attempt to provide an easily understandable ethical framework that could establish the rule of law as distinct from the rule of 'God' and Christian morality. His seminal work, *The Province of Jurisprudence Determined*, paved the way for the more recent development of the school of analytical jurisprudence.

53 Sir William Henry Rattigan (1842–1904) was a British judge and Liberal Unionist MP for North-East Lanarkshire. He served as judge in the Chief Court of Punjab on four occasions, was knighted in 1895, took silk in 1897 and practised in the high court of the NWP. He was also an additional member of the Supreme legislative council of India 1892–1893 and member of the Punjab legislative council 1898–1899. Sir Rattigan had also authored four books on law: *The Roman Law of Persons*, 1873; *The Science of Jurisprudence*, 1892; *Private International Law*, 1895; and *Digest of Customary Law for Punjab*, 1895.

54 *Kaisar-i-Hind*, translating to 'emperor' was a medal awarded to a person who distinguished himself/herself by important and useful service in the advancement of the public interest in India. Instituted by Queen Victoria on 10 April 1900, it ceased to be awarded following the passage of the Indian Independence Act, 1947. The awards were published in the *London Gazette* and the *Gazette of India*.

55 M. Hidayatullah, *My Own Boswell* (Nagpur: Universal Law Publishing House Lexis Nexis, 2016), 15.

56 *Aligarh Institute Gazette*. Aligarh, 9 September 1887.

57 'Letter of Syed Mahmood, Joint Secretary, MAO College Dated 15 June 1893, Addressed to Hon'ble Sir Syed Ahmad Khan, K.C.S.I. Life-Honorary Secretary, MAO College', *Aligarh Institute Gazette*, Aligarh, 20 June 1893.

58 Mehdi Manzil was used as the temporary law section at MAO. College. It is a lecture room in the east of Strachey Hall and was completed in 1882. It gets its name from Mohsin-ul-Mulk,

probably the closest associate of Sir Syed, who took over as the secretary of the college after Sir Syed's death.

59 Tahir Mahmood, *Reminiscing on Law Brains–Bench, Bar and Academia* (New Delhi: Universal Law Publishing Company, 2015), 32.

## CHAPTER 3 CAREER IN LAW AND AS A JUDGE

1 *Aligarh Institute Gazette*. Aligarh, 18 July 1887.

2 Supreme Court of India, *Courts of India: Past to Present* (New Delhi: Publication Division, Ministry of Information and Broadcasting, Government of India, 2016), 125.

3 Syed Mahmood, 'British Rule in India: Does It Owe Its Origin to Conquest, and Its Maintenance to Physical Force?', *The Calcutta Review* 68, (1879): 1.

4 Jon Wilson, 'The Temperament of Empire: Law and Conquest in Late Nineteenth Century India'. In *Subjects, Citizens and Law: Colonial and Postcolonial India*, eds. Gunnel Cederlof and Sanjukta Das Gupta (London: Routledge, 2016), 13.

5 Syed Mahmood, 'British Rule in India: Does It Owe Its Origin to Conquest, and Its Maintenance to Physical Force?', *Calcutta Review* 68, (1879): 2.

6 Ibid. 3.

7 Jon Wilson, 'The Temperament of Empire: Law and Conquest in Late Nineteenth Century India'. In *Subjects, Citizens and Law: Colonial and Postcolonial India*, eds. Gunnel Cederlof and Sanjukta Das Gupta (London: Routledge, 2016), 14.

8 Afzal Usmani, 'Justice Syed Mahmud', 2017. Available at: http://aligarhmovement.com/karwaan_e_aligarh/Justice_Syed_Mahmud (accessed on 16 March 2021).

9 Privy Council Appeal No 3 of 1882; (1884) Indian Law Reports 11 Privy Council 237. Date of District Court Judgement is 20 December 1880.

10 Para 1 of *Deputy Commissioner of Rae Bareli v. Rampal Singh*, Manupatra Online Legal Database/Privy Council/0045/1884.

11 *Centenary High Court of Judicature at Allahabad Commemoration 1866-1966*, Volume I, (Allahabad: Allahabad High Court Centenary Commemoration Volume Committee).

Available at: http://www.allahabadhighcourt.in/event/MrJusticeMahmoodGDSrivastava.pdf (accessed on 12 April 2021).

12 George Farquhar Irving Graham, *The Life and Work of Sir Syed Ahmed Khan C.S.I.* (Delhi: Idarah-i- Adabiyat-i-Delli, 1885), 262.

13 Letter by Syed Mahmood, Raebareli, to Sir Richard Meade, British Resident at Hyderabad, 29 January 1881, *Salar Jung Personal Papers*, vol. 2, Accession No. 751, (Hyderabad: Andhra Pradesh Provincial Archives), 1874–1884.

14 Letter from the Marquis of Ripon, Simla, to the Marquis of Hartington dated 25 August 1882; Letter from the Marquis of Ripon, Simla, to the Marquis of Hartington dated 31 August 1882; nos. 52 and 53 of Letters to the Secretary of State for India, Commencing from January 1882, The Marquis of Ripon; Correspondence with the Secretary of State for India in England, Ripon Collection, B.P. 7/3, 1882, British Library.

15 *Aligarh Institute Gazette*, Aligarh, 6 May 1882.

16 *Indu Prakash*, 3 March 1884. In Report on Native Papers, Public Bombay Presidency and Berar for the week ending 8 March 1884 in South Asian Open Archives. Available at: https://www.jstor.org/stable/10.2307/saoa.crl.25606000 (accessed on 2 February 2021).

17 (1884) Indian Law Reports 6 Allahabad 351.

18 Page 355 of the *Ishri v. Gopal Saran*, (1884) Indian Law Reports 6 Allahabad 351.

19 (1828) 26 United States 351.

20 (1886) Indian Law Reports 8 Allahabad 475.

21 Para 7 of *Mangulal and others v. Kandhai Lal and another*, Manupatra Online Legal Database/Uttar Pradesh/0123/1886.

22 (1886) Indian Law Reports 9 Allahabad 74.

23 An unconscionable bargain is one in which 'no man in his senses and not under delusions would make on one hand and no honest and fair man would accept on the other'. Under the law of contract, this principle is applied to set aside contracts in which a party to the contract appears to the court 'poor and ignorant', and the terms of the contract are substantially disadvantageous to him. A rebuttable presumption of law arises that the consent of such party was not free, i.e. presence of

some element vitiating consent. For instance, a very high rate of interest on the loan amount or any unreasonable pecuniary obligation, indicates the inequality in the bargaining power of the parties to a contract.

24 Para 1 of *Lalli v. Ram Prasad*, Manupatra Online Legal Database/Uttar Pradesh /0019/1886.

25 Para 11 of *Lalli v. Ram Prasad*, Manupatra Online Legal Database/Uttar Pradesh /0019/1886.

26 *Malik Rehmat v. Shiva Prasad*, (1891) Indian Law Reports 13 Allahabad 533.

27 Amar Nath Varma, 'The 125th Milestone: A Retrospect'. Available at: http://www.allahabadhighcourt.in/event/The125thMilestoneANVarma.html (accessed on 19 April 2021).

28 (1891) Indian Law Reports 13 Allahabad 171. For a detailed analysis of the judgment, see Chapter 4: Landmark Judgments of this book.

29 Justice Vaidyanathapuram Rama Krishna Iyer (1915–2014) was a multifaceted personality with inimitable qualities of judgeship and is often referred to as a conscience keeper of justice in India. He served as the judge of the Supreme Court of India for almost eight years (1973–1980), where he reformed the Indian justice system and stood up for the poor and underprivileged.

30 Justice Vaidyanathapuram Rama Krishna Iyer, 'Justice Mahmood's Relevance and Greatness'. In *Aligarh Law Journal*, 5 (1973): 68–69.

31 The word 'court' under Section 13 of the Statute 24 and 25 Victoria, Chapter 104 and Section 27 of the Letter of Patents, was construed to mean the 'Whole Court' by Justice Mahmood while Sir John interpreted it to mean only the chief justice or any other judge or bench nominated/assigned by the chief justice.

32 Syed Mahmood, 'Justice Syed Mahmood's letter dated 8 September 1893 addressed to Hon'ble J.D. La Touche, Chief Secretary to the Government of NWP and Oudh'. In *Justice Syed Mahmood Papers*, ed. Iqbal Husain, (Aligarh Muslim University, Aligarh: Sir Syed Academy, 2005).

33 (1888) Indian Law Reports 10 Allahabad 289. The judgment has been discussed in detail in Chapter 4: Landmark Judgments of this book.

34 (1891) Indian Law Reports 13 Allahabad 537.

35 (1892) Indian Law Reports 14 Allahabad 273. The judgment has been discussed in detail in Chapter 4: Landmark Judgments of this book.

36 Justice Syed Mahmood's letter dated 30 October 1892 addressed to the Hon'ble Chief Secretary NWP.

37 Justice Syed Mahmood's letter dated 30 October 1892 and reply of Sir John dated 2 August 1892.

38 Sir John John's letter dated 7 July 1893 addressed to the chief secretary of the NWP Government.

39 Ibid.

40 'Quarrel between the Chief Justice and Mr. Justice Mahmood Regarding the Muharram Holidays', *The Najmul Akhbar*, Etawah, 10 August 1892.

41 Syed Mahmood, 'Justice Syed Mahmood's Letter Dated 8 September 1893 Addressed to Hon'ble J.D. La Touche, Chief Secretary to the Government of NWP and Oudh'. In *Justice Syed Mahmood Papers*, ed. Iqbal Husain (Aligarh Muslim University, Aligarh: Sir Syed Academy, 2005), 67-68.

42 The judgements referred here are in reference to the cases heard by the two-judge (miscellaneous) bench comprising Justice Mahmood and Chief Justice Sir John, or where the case was heard by the full bench of the high court. *Muhammad Allahadad Khan v. Ismail Khan*, (1888) Indian Law Reports 10 Allahabad 289 and *Wali Ahmad Khan v. Ajudhia Kandu*, (1891) Indian Law Reports 13 Allahabad 537 and *Seth Bhitor Mal v. Shib Lal*, (1892) Indian Law Reports 14 Allahabad 273.

43 '*Veni, Vidi, Vici*' is a Latin phrase meaning 'I came, I saw, I conquered'. It was first used by the famous Roman emperor Julius Caesar after he won a battle in Asia Minor (now Turkey).

44 'Justice Syed Mahmood's Letter Dated 30 October 1892 Addressed to Hon'ble J.D. La Touche, Chief Secretary to the Government of NWP and Oudh', 64.

45 'Sir John Edge's Letter Dated 7 July 1893 Addressed to J.D. La Touche, Chief Secretary of the Government, NWP and Oudh as reported in *Justice Syed Mahmood Papers*, ed. Iqbal Husain, (Aligarh Muslim University, Aligarh: Sir Syed Academy, 2005), 62.

46 Syed Mahmood, 'Justice Syed Mahmood's Letter Dated 8 September 1893 Addressed to Hon'ble J.D. La Touche, Chief Secretary to the Government of NWP and Oudh'. In *Justice Syed Mahmood Papers*, ed. Iqbal Husain, (Aligarh Muslim University, Aligarh: Sir Syed Academy, 2005), 44–46.

47 Ibid. 67.

48 Ibid. 65–66.

49 Para 42 of Justice Syed Mahmood's letter dated 8 September 1893 addressed to Hon'ble J.D. La Touche, chief secretary to the Government of NWP and Oudh.

50 In the same letter, he also prayed for the acceptance of his resignation from service.

51 An enactment for regulating enquires into the behaviour of public servants.

52 He had to take a year-long furlough as a venomous insect had inflicted a wound on his left leg causing foot ulcer, which was operated by Dr E.A. Mapleton and I.F. Tuoby of Allahabad. Post surgery, he had great difficulty in walking and keeping his foot on the ground.

53 Shafey Kidwai, *Sir Syed Ahmad Khan: Reason, Religion and Nation* (India: Routledge, 2021), 30–31.

54 *Centenary High Court of Judicature at Allahabad Commemoration 1866-1966*, Volume. Allahabad: Allahabad High Court Centenary Commemoration Volume Committee, Volume I. *Available at*: http://www.allahabadhighcourt.in/event/Justice_Syed_Mahmood_M_Hidayatullah.pdf (accessed on 22 April 2021).

55 Para 62 of Justice Syed Mahmood's letter dated 8 September 1893 addressed to Hon'ble J.D. La Touche, chief secretary to the Government of NWP and Oudh.

56 *The Hindustani*. Lucknow, 12 October 1892. In *Selections from the Vernacular Newspapers Published in the Panjab, NWP, Oudh, Central Provinces and Berar*. Available at: https://www.jstor.org/stable/10.2307/saoa.crl.25007335 (accessed on 28 January 2021).

57 Anwar Masood, 'And the End of Mahmood Came', *Aligarh Law Journal*, 5 (1973): 301.

58 Shamsur Rahman Faruqi, *From Antiquity to Social Revolutionary: Sir Syed Ahmad Khan and the Colonial Experience*, (AMU, Aligarh: Sir Syed Academy, 2007), 7.

59 *Halat-i-Hind*, Allahabad, 3 February 1892. In *Selections from the Vernacular Newspapers Published in the Panjab, NWP, Oudh, Central Provinces and Berar.* Available at: https://www.jstor.org/stable/10.2307/saoa.crl.24998521 (accessed on 22 March 2021).

60 Raja Ajit Singh was, at that time, 74 years old. He was an old *taluqdar* who enjoyed a respectable position in British India. He paid more than a lakh rupees per annum as revenue to the government and also exercised the powers of assistant commissioner.

61 *Azad*, Lucknow, 4 March 1888. In *Selections from the Vernacular Newspapers published in the Panjab, North-Western Provinces, Oudh, Central Provinces and Berar.* Available at: https://www.jstor.org/stable/10.2307/saoa.crl.24997881 (Accessed on 11 February 2021).

62 The Lady Justice, also known as *Justitia*, is a metaphorical personification of the moral force in judicial systems.

63 Tahir Mahmood, *Reminiscing on Law Brains – Bench, Bar and* Academia (New Delhi: Universal Law Publishing Company, 2015), 33.

64 *Wakf* means the permanent dedication by a person professing Islam, of any movable or immovable property for any purpose recognised by the Muslim law as pious, religious or charitable. Where the *wakf* is created for the benefit of the *wakif*'s children and their offsprings, it is termed as *wakf-alal-aulad*. The beneficiaries are entitled to derive benefit from the usufruct of the *wakf* property but are not vested with the right to alienate the corpus of such property.

65 Hafeez Malik, 'Sir Sayyid Ahmad Khan's Contribution to the Development of Muslim Nationalism in India', *Modern Asian Studies*, 4, no. 2, (1970):134.

66 Lucy Caroll, 'Life Interests and Inter-Generational Transfer of Property Avoiding the Law of Succession', *Islamic Law and Society* 8, no. 2, (2001): 262.

67 Sir Frederick Pollock, *The Law of Torts: A Treatise on the Principles of Obligations arising from Civil Wrongs in the Common Law: to which is added the Draft of a Code of Civil Wrongs prepared for the Government of India* (London: Stevens and Sons, 1895).

68 Statute 24 and 25 Victoria C. 104 and provided for the extension of the territorial jurisdiction of the high courts that existed in India.

69 Minute by Justice Mahmood on High Courts Bill, 1888. 4 February 1889. In Government of India, Home Judicial, May 1889, no. 236–261.

70 Minutes by Justice Mahmood on the Guardians and Wards' Bill (No. II), 19 April 1890. In NWP and Oudh, Judicial (Civil) Department Proceedings, 32–38.

71 *Alam-i-Taswir*, Cawnpore, 16 August 1892. In *Selections from the Vernacular Newspapers Published in the Panjab, NWP, Oudh, Central Provinces and Berar*. Available at: https://www.jstor.org/stable/10.2307/saoa.crl.25007328 (accessed on 11 March 2021).

## CHAPTER 4 LANDMARK JUDGMENTS

1 Three hundred and fourteen of these 383 judgments are available on the online legal database *Manupatra*. Available at: http://www.manupatrafast.in (accessed on 16 April 2021).

2 This is an approximate number based on manual perusal of Indian Law Reports and legal databases by the authors.

3 *Centenary High Court of Judicature at Allahabad Commemoration 1866-1966*, Volume. Allahabad: Allahabad High Court Centenary Commemoration Volume Committee.
Available at: http://www.allahabadhighcourt.in/event/Speech_by_Hon_K_Subbarao27-11-66.pdf (accessed on 18 April 2021).

4 Sir Whitley Stokes, *The Anglo-Indian Codes* (Oxford: Clarendon Press, 1887), xxviii.

5 Justice Vaidyanathapuram Rama Iyer Krishna Iyer, 'Justice Mahmood's Relevance and Greatness', *Aligarh Law Journal*, 5 (1973): 68–69.

6 (1891) Indian Law Reports 13 Allahabad 171.

7 Professor B.B. Pande, 'Expanding Horizons of Criminal Procedural Law', *Supreme Court Cases* 2, no. 1 (2021): 81.

8 Para 32 of *Queen Empress v. Pohpi*, Manupatra Online Legal Database/Uttar Pradesh/0048/1891.

9 Para 48 and 49 of *Queen Empress v. Pohpi*, Manupatra Online Legal Database/Uttar Pradesh/0048/1891.

10 2018 Supreme Court Cases OnLine, Uttarakhand 1270.

11 Justice Manepalli Narayana Rao Venkatachaliah, 'Keeping the Spirit of the Common Law Alive', *National University Juridical Sciences Law Review* 5, no. 3 (2012): 299.

12 *Indian People*, Allahabad Issue, 23 June 1907. In *Selections from the Native Newspapers Published in the United Provinces of Agra and Oudh*. Available at: https://www.jstor.org/stable/10.2307/saoa.crl.26079580.

13 (1884) Indian Law Reports 6 Allahabad 509.

14 The Indian Evidence Act, 1872 (Act 01 of 1872).

15 (1890) Indian Law Reports 12 Allahabad 79.

16 Code of Civil Procedure, 1882 and the Limitation Act, 1877.

17 *Centenary High Court of Judicature at Allahabad 1866-1966 Commemoration Volume*, 1966. Allahabad: Allahabad High Court Centenary Commemoration Volume Committee, Volume II. Available at: http://www.allahabadhighcourt.in/event/Justice_Syed_Mahmood_M_Hidayatullah.pdf. (accessed on 19 March 2021)

18 Letter from Syed Mahmood, District Judge, Bareli addressed to Lt. Col. P.D. Henderson, general superintendent of Operations for the Suppression of Thuggee and Dacoity dated 15 June 1881, included as an enclosure in Letter from the Marquis of Ripon, Simla, to the Marquis of Hartington, 15 July. 1881, No. 35 of Letters from the Secretary of State for India to the Viceroy, Commencing from January 1881, The Marquis of Ripon, Correspondence with the Secretary of State for India in England, Ripon Collection, B.P. 7/3, 1881, British Library.

19 (1885) Indian Law Reports 7 Allahabad 822.

20 (1885) Indian Law Reports 7 Allahabad 775.

21 Para 799 of *Gobind Dayal v. Inayatullah* (1885) Indian Law Reports 7 Allahabad 775.

22 The 'pre-emptor' is the owner of the property adjacent to the property sold to a third party without the offer of sale being first made to him.

23 The 'vendor' is the seller of the property in question.

24 The 'vendee' of the property is the buyer of the property.

25 All Indian Reporter 2020 Supreme Court 782.

26 (1885) Indian Law Reports 7 Allahabad 775.

27 (2017) 9 Supreme Court Cases 1.

28 Para 420 of *Shayara Bano v. Union of India*, Manupatra Online Legal Database/Supreme Court/1031/2017.

29 The word *amin* or *aameen* is of Semitic origin, being used both in Arabic and Hebrew, and has been adopted in prayers by Muhammadans as much as by Christians. The word does not occur in the Koran, but in conformity with the *sunnah* or the practice of the Prophet, it is regarded by Muhammadans as an essential part of the prayers, as a word representing earnestness in devotion. The word is pronounced at the end of the first chapter of the Koran.

30 At what note of the vocal octave the voice on saying *amin* should emanate?

31 Section 296–Disturbing Religious Assembly: Whoever voluntarily causes disturbance to any assembly lawfully engaged in the performance of religious worship, or religious ceremonies, shall be punished with imprisonment of either description for a term which may extend to one year, or with fine, or with both.

32 (1891) Indian Law Reports 13 Allahabad 419.

33 (1885) Indian Law Reports 7 Allahabad 461.

34 Para 18 *Jangu v. Ahmad Ullah*, Manupatra Online Legal Database/Uttar Pradesh/0004/1889.

35 (1890) Indian Law Reports 12 Allahabad 494.

36 (1891) Indian Law Reports 13 Allahabad 419.

37 (1885) Indian Law Reports 7 Allahabad 461.

38 Para 10 of *Ata-Ullah and another v. Azim-Ullah and another*, Manupatra Online Legal Database/Uttar Pradesh/0052/1889.

39 (1888) Indian Law Reports 10 Allahabad 289.

40 Para 17 of *Muhammad Allahadad Khan v. Muhammad Ismail Khan*, Manupatra Online legal Database/Uttar Pradesh/0012/1888.

41 Section 112 of the Indian Evidence Act 1872—Birth during marriage, conclusive proof of legitimacy.

The fact that any person was born during the continuance of a valid marriage between his mother and any man, or within 280 days after its dissolution, the mother remaining unmarried, shall be conclusive proof that he is the legitimate son of that man, unless it can be shown that the parties to the marriage had no access to each other at any time when he could have been begotten.

42 Justice Vaidyanathapuram Rama Iyer Krishna Iyer, 'Justice Mahmood's Relevance and Greatness', *Aligarh Law Journal*, 5 (1973): 70.

43 Sohaira Siddiqui, 'Navigating Colonial Power: Challenging Precedents and the Limitation of Local Elites', *Islamic Law and Society* 26, no.3 (2018): 41.

44 Ibid. 37–38

45 Ibid. 38.

46 (1886) Indian Law Reports 8 Allahabad 149.

47 The Tagore Law Lectures, instituted in 1868, were organised by the University of Calcutta during British India. They were considered the most prestigious series of lectures in the field of law.

48 Para 8 of *Abdul Kadir v. Salima*, Manupatra Online Legal Database/Uttar Pradesh/0065/1886.

49 Para 12 of *Abdul Kadir v. Salima*, Manupatra Online Legal Database/Uttar Pradesh/0065/1886.

50 Para 12 of *Abdul Kadir v. Salima*, Manupatra Online Legal Database/Uttar Pradesh/0065/1886.

51 Asaf Ali Asghar Fyzee, *Cases in the Muhammadan Law of India, Pakistan and Bangladesh*, (Oxford University Press, 1965).

52 (1884) Indian Law Reports 7 Allahabad 297. The maxim is mentioned in Para 2 of *Mazhar Ali v. Budh Singh*, Manupatra Online Legal Database/Uttar Pradesh/0051/1884.

53 Para 11 of *Mazhar Ali v. Budh Singh*, Manupatra Online Legal Database/Uttar Pradesh/0051/1884.

54 Para 2 of *Mazhar Ali v. Budh Singh*, Manupatra Online Legal Database/Uttar Pradesh/0051/1884.

55 (1889) Indian Law Reports 11 Allahabad 194.

56 Professor Virendra Singh Rekhi, 'Mahmood's Opinion in the Janki Case: A Study in Activism', *Aligarh Law Journal*, 5 (1973): 130.

57 (1891) Indian Law Reports 13 Allahabad 126.

58 *Moonshee Buzloor Ruheem v. Shamsoon Nisa*, 11 M.I.A. 551.

59 Manusmriti (Sanskrit: 'Laws of Manu' or 'The Remembered Tradition of Manu'), also called Manava-dharma-shastra ('The Dharma Text of Manu'), is traditionally the most authoritative of the books of the Hindu code (Dharma-shastra) in India. It is

attributed to the legendary first man in the Hindu mythology and lawgiver, Manu. The received text dates from circa 100 CE.

60 Written by the Sage Harita, *Harita Smriti* is a work on Hindu law.

61 *Lichita Smriti* is told in 93 verses by Sage Lichita. Sage Lichita is considered an authority by the followers of Shukla Yajurvedins.

62 The foundation of this right is the fundamental rule of matrimonial law that one spouse is entitled to the society/consortium of other, and where one spouse has abandoned or withdrawn from the society of the other without reasonable excuse or just cause, the court should grant a decree for restitution.

63 (1882) Indian Law Reports 4 Allahabad 532.

64 Para 16 *Indar Kaur v. Lalta Prasad Singh*, Manupatra Online Legal Database/Uttar Pradesh/0075/1882

65 (1886) Indian Law Reports 9 Allahabad 253.

66 (1892) Indian Law Reports 14 Allahabad 67 (Full Bench).

67 *Factum valet* means the act which should not be done is valid when it is done. While enforcing Hindu Law, the British Courts enforced the doctrine of *factum valet* under the sweep of equity, justice and good conscience. This doctrine is applicable when there is obligation and not the legal prohibition for a thing. In other words, if the act is accomplished and eventually completed, the action will be considered lawful and binding.

68 Para 88 of *Beni Prasad v. Hardai Bibi and Others*, Manupatra Online Legal Database/Uttar Pradesh/0071/1892.

69 (1884) Indian Law Reports 7 Allahabad 313

70 Para 23 of *Kandhiya Lal v. Chandra and Others*, Manupatra Online Legal Database/Uttar Pradesh/0052/1884.

71 (1892) Indian Law Reports 14 Allahabad 273.

72 The law of salvage is a principle of Maritime Law whereby any person who helps recover another person's ship or cargo in peril at sea is entitled to a reward commensurate with the value of the property salved.

73 Page 320 of *Chittor Mal v. Shib Lal* (1892) Indian Law Reports 14 Allahabad 273.

74 Procedural law refers to the law that establishes the rules of the court and the methods used to ensure the rights of parties in the

court system. In particular, they provide how the business of the court is to be conducted.

75 (1883) Indian Law Reports 5 Allahabad 163.

76 Para 5 of *Narsingh Das v. Mangal Dubey and Others*, Manupatra Online Legal Database/Uttar Pradesh/0084/1882.

77 (1885) Indian Law Reports 7 Allahabad 606.

78 Generally, a judgment of a court has two parts—obiter dictum and ratio decidendi. Obiter dictum is a mere opinion which is unnecessary for the decision of the case. On the other hand, ratio decidendi constitutes the ground or reason for the decision of the case.

79 Para 10 of *Lutfunnissa v. Jamiatunnissa*, Manupatra Online Legal Database/Uttar Pradesh/0066/1885

80 Editor. 1930. "Law Reports" *Madras Law Journal- Civil Journal Article*, Volume I: 121. Lexis Nexis India.
https://advance.lexis.com/api/permalink/118a4473-3e94-472f-aeb4-2c7d67810c9c/?context=1523890

81 (1886) Indian Law Reports 8 Allahabad 282.

82 Para 8 of *Muhammad Salim v. Nabian Bibi and Others*, Manupatra Online Legal Database/Uttar Pradesh/0091/1886

83 Para 6 of *Muhammad Salim v. Nabian Bibi and Others*, Manupatra Online Legal Database/Uttar Pradesh/0091/1886

84 (1883) Indian Law Reports 5 Allahabad 121.

85 It translates to bare ownership. It is used to denote the property where the owner only has the title to the property but not the possession of it.

86 *Emphytusis or Emphyteusis* refers to a continual right in a property that belongs to another. In other words, the right of a person who is not the owner of a piece of land, to use it as his own in perpetuity, subject to forfeiture on non-payment of a fixed rent, and on certain other contingencies.

87 Para 14 of *Gopal Pandey and Others. v. Parsotam Das and Others*, Manupatra Online Legal Database/Uttar Pradesh/0081/1882.

88 Law Commission of India. 1977. *70th Report on the Transfer of Property Act, 1882*. New Delhi: Ministry of Law, Justice and Company Affairs.
Available at: https://lawcommissionofindia.nic.in/51-100/Report70.pdf (accessed on 27 February 2021).

89 (1891) Indian Law Reports, 13 Allahabad 432 (Full Bench).

90 Law Commission of India, *70th Report on the Transfer of Property Act, 1882* (New Delhi: Ministry of Law, Justice and Company Affairs, 1977), Para 1. 20.

91 (1890) Indian Law Reports 12 Allahabad 1.

92 Law Commission of India, *69th Report on the Indian Evidence Act, 1872* (New Delhi: Ministry of Law, Justice and Company Affairs, 1977).
Available at: https://lawcommissionofindia.nic.in/51-100/Report69.pdf (accessed on 8 March 2021)

93 Law Commission of India, *69th Report on the Indian Evidence Act, 1872* (New Delhi: Ministry of Law, Justice and Company Affairs, 1977), para 8.73.

94 *Queen Empress v. Pohpi* in *Abdul Majid v. State* The All Pakistan Law Decisions 1973 Lahore 448 and *Dr. Ejaz Hussain Qureshi and Another v. Government of Punjab and two others* The All Pakistan Law Decisions 1978 Lahore 1419.
*Chittor Mal v. Shib Lal* in Haji Nizam Khan v. Additional District Judge, Lyallpur and Other The All Pakistan Law Decisions 1976 Lahore 930.
*Ishri v. Gopal Saran* in *Muhammad Afzal and 8 others v. Haji Fazal-ul-Haq and Another* The All Pakistan Law Decisions 1971 Supreme Court 162 and *Republic of India through Deputy High Commissioner, Lahore v. Messrs Chiragh Din and Company* The All Pakistan Law Decisions 1975 Lahore 1047.

95 *Gobind Dayal v. Inayatullah* in *Onil Kuar Podder and Others v. Mostafa Unuch* (2015) 67 Dhaka Law Reports 302.

96 *Palakdhari Singh v. The Collector of Gorakhpur and Others* in *Canyong Packing Sdn Bhd v. Puah Keh Ming and Anor 2018 Malayan Law Journal* 738.

97 *Mazhar Ali v. Budh Singh* in *Hakam Bibi v. Mistry Fateh Mohd* (1951) 28 Kenya Law Reports 91.

## CHAPTER 5 ENGAGEMENTS AFTER RESIGNATION FROM JUDGESHIP AND LAST DAYS

1 Syed Mahmood, *A History of English Education in India–Its Rise, Development, Progress, Present Condition and Prospects being a Narrative of the Various Phases of Educational Policy and Measures Adopted under the British Rule from its*

*Beginning to the Present Period* (Delhi: Idarah-I-Adabiyat-i Delli, 1895), iii.

2 Rehmani Begum Mohammad Ruknuddin Hassan, 'The Educational Movement of Sir Syed Ahmad Khan 1858-1898' (Unpublished PhD Thesis: School of Oriental and African Studies, University of London, London, 1959), 443.

3 Syed Mahmood, *A History of English Education in India* (Delhi: Idarah-I-Adabiyat-i Delli, 1895), 54.

4 Abdul Rashid Khan, *All India Muslim Educational Conference: Its Contribution to the Cultural Development of Indian Muslims* (Pakistan: Oxford, 2001).

5 Syed Mahmood, *A History of English Education in India* (Delhi: Idarah-I-Adabiyat-i Delli, 1895), ii.

6 Ibid. 246.

7 William Hunter, *Report of the Indian Education Commission* (Calcutta: Superintendent of Government Printing, 1883).

8 *Aligarh Institute Gazette*. Aligarh, 30 October 1886.

9 It was Lord Lytton who vouched for Mahmood's appointment as a judge as discussed in Chapter 3 of this book.

10 William Hunter, *Report on the Indian Education Commission* (Calcutta: Superintendent of Government Printing Press, 1883), 597–598.

11 Shan Muhammad, *Writings and Speeches of Sir Syed Ahmad Khan* (Bombay: Nachiketa Publications Limited, 1972).

12 S. Chaudhary, 'Language Education, Language Modernisation and Globalisation'. In *Language Education in Multilingual India*, ed. Chander J. Daswani (Regional Bureau for Communication and Information in Asia and the Pacific New Delhi: UNESCO, 2001), 151–183.
Available at: https://unesdoc.unesco.org/ark:/48223/pf0000125246 (accessed on 11 April 2021)

13 Syed Mahmood, 'Syed Mahmood's Letter Dated July 1898'. In *Justice Syed Mahmood Papers*, ed. Iqbal Husain (Aligarh Muslim University, Aligarh: Sir Syed Academy, 2005), 205.

14 Shafey Kidwai, *Sir Syed Ahmad Khan-Religion, Reason and Nation* (India: Routledge India, 2021), 31.

15 *Aligarh Institute Gazette*. Aligarh, 6 April 1894.
The *Aligarh Institute Gazette* dated 6 April 1894 notified to the public constitution of the Muhammadan Anglo-Oriental

Defence Association of Upper India. The Association had the following objects: To protect the political interests of the Muhammadans by representing their views before the English people and the Indian government;
to discourage popular political agitation amongst Muhammadans;
to lend its support to measures calculated to increase the stability of the British government and the security of the Empire; to strive to preserve peace in India; and to encourage sentiments of loyalty in the population;
Membership: All persons sympathising with the objects of the Association could become members on payment of an annual subscription fee of ₹ 3.
No person who was a paid government servant or who was in statu pupillari could be admitted to the membership of the Association.
Governance and Policy Making: The policy of the Association was directed by the Council, which had the entire charge of its business.
Syed Mahmood, Theodore Morrison and 10 others were the members of its founding Council.

16 *Aligarh Institute Gazette*. Aligarh, 28 January 1896.

17 Alan Guenther, 'Syed Mahmood and the Transformation of Muslim Law in British India', (Unpublished PhD thesis: Institute of Islamic Studies, McGill University, Canada, 2004), 91–92.

18 Syed Mahmood, 'Syed Mahmood's Letter Dated 8 September 1893 Addressed to Hon'ble J.D. La Touche, Chief Secretary to the Government of NWP and Oudh'. In *Justice Syed Mahmood Papers*, ed. Iqbal Husain (Aligarh Muslim University, Aligarh: Sir Syed Academy, 2005), 59–60.

19 Ibid.

20 Shyam Krishna Bhatnagar, *History of the M.A.O. College* (AMU, Aligarh: Sir Syed Hall Publication, 1969), 15.

21 Details of the controversy have been mentioned by Syed Mahmood in his letter dated 1 December 1898 addressed to Theodore Beck Esquire, principal and registrar, MAO College, Aligarh published in Khalique Ahmad Nizami,

*Theodore Beck Papers from the Sir Syed Academy Archives* (Aligarh: Aligarh Muslim University Press, 1991).

22 Theodore Beck, 'Theodore Beck's Letter Dated 19 March 1896 Addressed to the Hon'ble Sir Syed Ahmed Khan, Bahadur, K.C.S.I., LL.D'. In *Theodore Beck Papers from Sir Syed Academy Archives*, ed. K.A. Nizami, (Aligarh Muslim University, Aligarh: Sir Syed Academy, 1991), 300.

23 Ibid.

24 Theodore Beck, 'Theodore Beck's Letter Dated 22 July 1899 Addressed to Nawab Mohsin-ul-Mulk'. In *Theodore Beck Papers from Sir Syed Academy Archives*, ed. K.A. Nizami, (Aligarh Muslim University, Aligarh: Sir Syed Academy, 1991), 381.

25 Ibid. 382.

26 Shyam Krishna Bhatnagar, *History of the M.A.O. College*, (AMU, Aligarh: Sir Syed Hall Publication, 1969), 114–121.

27 Ibid. 172–173.

28 Saeed-un-Nisa Begum was the wife of Syed Muhammad Ahmad.

29 Arshad Masood, 'And the End of Mahmood Came', *Aligarh Law Journal*, 5 (1973): 304.

30 A 'quatrain' is a rhymed grouping of four lines in a poem. It can be a poem that has only four lines, or it can be a stanza in a longer poem.

31 Moulvi Ghulam Muhammad alias Hadi Ali Khan.

32 The Holy Koran, Chapter 12.

33 The Holy Koran, Chapter 12, Verse 156.

## CHAPTER 6 SHAPING INTERFAITH DEBATE

1 Brojendra Mitter, *Indian Judges: Biographical and Critical Sketches with Portraits* (Madras: G.A. Natesan and Company, 1932), 322.

2 George Farquhar Irving Graham, *The Life and Work of Sir Syed Ahmed Khan C.S.I.*, (Delhi: Idarah-i-Adabiyat-i-Delli, 1885), 251.

3 *Aligarh Institute Gazette*. Aligarh, 9 May 1882.

4 Syed Mahmood, 'A Scheme for the Proposed Muhammadan Anglo-Oriental College dated 10 February 1873'. In *Syed Mahmood Papers* (AMU, Aligarh: Sir Syed Academy, 2005), 229.

5 Ibid. 233.
6 Ibid. 226.
7 Mohammad Ameen Zuberi, *Tazkira-e-Syed Mahmood* (Aligarh: Institute Press, year not known), 51.
8 Syed Mahmood, 'British Rule in India: Does it owe its origin to Conquest, and its maintenance to physical force?', *The Calcutta Review* 68 (1879): 17.
9 Ibid. 15.
10 Ibid. 16.
11 Ibid.
12 'Vice Chancellor Professor Tariq Mansoor's Address Dated 22 December 2020, Delivered During the Centenary Celebration Programme'. *Aligarh Institute Gazette-Centenary Special Issue* (AMU, Aligarh: Sir Syed Academy, 2020), 36.
13 'Syed Mahmood's Address Dated 9 January 1877, Delivered at the Foundation Stone Laying Ceremony of MAO College, Aligarh In *Justice Syed Mahmood Papers*, ed. Iqbal Husain, (Aligarh Muslim University, Aligarh: Sir Syed Academy, 2005), 356.
14 Para 147 of *Beni Prasad v. Hardai Bibi*, Manupatra Online Legal Database/Uttar Pradesh/0071/1892.
15 Sunil Ambwani, 'Contribution of the Allahabad High Court to the Development of Law', Paper presented at the High Court Justices' Conference on the Contribution of Indian High Courts to the Development of Law (Bhopal: National Judicial Academy, 14–16 March 2008).

# INDEX

## ABOUT MOHAMMAD NASIR

MOHAMMAD NASIR is Assistant Professor in the Department of Law, Aligarh Muslim University. He has taught as a visiting faculty at the Indian Institute of Management, Uttarakhand. His academic interests lie in business law, law and development and legal reform, through which he seeks to empower the marginalised. His opinion pieces on legal and socio-political issues have been carried by the *Hindustan Times*, *Indian Express*, *Wire* and *OPEN*.

On the centenary of AMU, he contributed to 'A History of Aligarh Muslim University 1920-2020' published by the *Times of India*, and co-edited the Special Centenary Issue of the *Aligarh Institute Gazette*, a periodical started by AMU founder Sir Syed in 1866.

His presentation on how governance reforms in panchayati raj institutions can mitigate India's disequalising development pattern was awarded 2nd best at the National University of Juridical Sciences, Kolkata (India) in 2012. He spoke on India's mandatory Corporate Social Responsibility regime at Edinburgh, Scotland in 2014, and against India's retentionist position on death penalty at Keble College, University of Oxford in 2016. The National Legal Services Authority of India published his contribution on Property Rights of Women under Muslim Law in its module for 'Training of Legal Services Lawyers' with a foreword by the Chief Justice of India. He has worked in the office of the Additional Solicitor General of India (Supreme Court) on the Indian government's gas pricing policy in 2011.

In the corporate and institutional life of AMU, he is a member of the Institutional Ethics Committee of Jawaharlal Nehru Medical College, the University Ranking committee and the governing body of Dara Shikoh Centre for Interfaith Dialogue & Understanding.

A gold medallist in the All-India Inter-University Lawn Tennis Championship 2013 representing AMU, he was awarded the Certificate of Outstanding Merit by AMU for his extra-curricular contributions to the university in 2011.

## ABOUT SAMREEN AHMED

SAMREEN AHMED is a legal researcher and writer based at the Aligarh Muslim University. Her research interests are in legal history, women and law, and intellectual property law. Her academic writings have been published in the *Economic & Political Weekly*. A recipient of Obaid Bin Saif Al-Nasseri Gold Medal, University Gold Medal, Dr Ghoolam Vahanvati Gold Medal in law from AMU, she is also passionately engaged in empowering destitute women through skill development in Uttar Pradesh.